The Hero Maker

Learn how to turn your school board members into heroes by helping them make smart, worthwhile decisions they will deserve to brag about. In this much-needed book, Ryan Donlan and Todd Whitaker offer practical strategies to help superintendents develop better working relationships with their boards.

You'll discover how to:

- ◆ reconnect board members to the real purpose of education, despite their personal agendas
- ◆ work with your board more effectively during meetings and at times in between
- ◆ guide board members into more productive roles when they overreach beyond policymaking
- ◆ connect and communicate with board members regardless of personal disposition

Each chapter contains hero-making tips to help you get started. In addition, this timely second edition features a new chapter on navigating the superintendent–board president relationship. With this practical book, you'll be able to overcome the challenges of the superintendent–board relationship so that your board can make better decisions for those who matter most—the students.

Ryan Donlan is a Professor of Educational Leadership at Indiana State University and specializes in school leadership, governance, and team performance, with books for board members, superintendents, principals, assistant principals, and teachers, including *Uncommon Sense for New Teachers: A Good Beginning is Half the Work*.

Todd Whitaker is a Research Professor at the University of Missouri. He is a leading presenter in the field of education and has written 65 books, including the national best seller, *What Great Teachers Do Differently*.

Also Available from Routledge Eye on Education
(www.routledge.com/k-12)

The School Board Member's Guidebook, 2nd Edition:
Making A Positive Difference Through School Governance
Ryan Donlan and Todd Whitaker

What Great Teachers Do Differently, 3rd Edition:
Nineteen Things That Matter Most
Todd Whitaker

What Great Principals Do Differently, 3rd Edition:
Twenty Things That Matter Most
Todd Whitaker

Leading School Change, 2nd Edition: How to Overcome
Resistance, Increase Buy-in, and Accomplish Your Goals
Todd Whitaker

Your First Year, 2nd Edition: How to Survive and Thrive as a
New Teacher
Todd Whitaker, Katherine Whitaker, and
Madeline Whitaker Good

Dealing with Difficult Parents (School Leader Edition):
How to Model, Coach, and Support Your Teachers
Todd Whitaker and Douglas Fiore

Dealing with Difficult Teachers, 3rd Edition
Todd Whitaker

Invest in Your Best: 9 Strategies to Grow, Support, and
Celebrate Your Most Valuable Teachers
Todd Whitaker, Connie Hamilton, Joseph Jones, and T.J. Vari

Turning It Around: Small Steps or Sweeping Changes to
Create the School Your Students Deserve
Todd Whitaker and Courtney Monterecy

The Hero Maker
How Superintendents Can Get Their School Boards to Do the Right Thing

Second Edition

Ryan Donlan and Todd Whitaker

NEW YORK AND LONDON

Second edition published 2026
by Routledge
605 Third Avenue, New York, NY 10158

and by Routledge
4 Park Square, Milton Park, Abingdon, Oxon, OX14 4RN

Routledge is an imprint of the Taylor & Francis Group, an informa business

© 2026 Ryan Donlan and Todd Whitaker

The right of Ryan Donlan and Todd Whitaker to be identified as authors of this work has been asserted in accordance with sections 77 and 78 of the Copyright, Designs and Patents Act 1988.

All rights reserved. No part of this book may be reprinted or reproduced or utilised in any form or by any electronic, mechanical, or other means, now known or hereafter invented, including photocopying and recording, or in any information storage or retrieval system, without permission in writing from the publishers.

Trademark notice: Product or corporate names may be trademarks or registered trademarks and are used only for identification and explanation without intent to infringe.

First edition published by Routledge 2017

ISBN: 978-1-041-01210-8 (hbk)
ISBN: 978-1-041-01207-8 (pbk)
ISBN: 978-1-003-61368-8 (ebk)

DOI: 10.4324/9781003613688

Typeset in Palatino
by codeMantra

Contents

Meet the Authors vi
Acknowledgments viii

Introduction... 1

1 The Hero Maker 9

2 Constituencies.. 17

3 The Board of Education............................. 27

4 The Superintendent as the Shield.................. 41

5 The Care and Feeding of Board Members.......... 47

6 Board Meetings....................................... 57

7 Between Board Meetings 67

8 The Superintendent–Board President Relationship 73

9 Advancing, by Retreating........................... 89

10 Board Personalities.................................. 97

11 Starting Undefeated.................................. 105

12 The Tour of Duty 111

Epilogue: What Next? Toward "Difference-Making" 119

Meet the Authors

Dr. Ryan Donlan helps leaders, teams, and organizations in all sectors toward personal and professional excellence. Schools, teachers, and school leaders are his focus. Ryan is a Professor of Educational Leadership in the Bayh College of Education at Indiana State University in Terre Haute, Indiana. He leverages leadership capacity in others toward higher performance. Prior to his university career, Ryan started as a high school teacher and served as an assistant principal, principal, and superintendent over many years. Leadership development, school reimagination, and organizational wellness are his specialties, as are human-behavior analysis, the study of personality and communication, and human development. With wide-ranging publications, Ryan is author/co-author of the books *Minds Unleashed: How Principals Can Lead the Right Brained Way*, *The School Board Member's Guidebook: Making A Positive Difference Through School Governance*, *All Other Duties as Assigned: The Assistant Principal's Critical Role in Supporting Schools Inside and Out*, *Ensuring Teachers Matter: Where to Focus First So Students Matter Most*, and *Uncommon Sense for New Teachers: A Good Beginning Is Half the Work*. Ryan is married to Wendy, a teacher in the Early Childhood Education Center at Indiana State University. They are the parents of two children, Sean and Katelyn.

Dr. Todd Whitaker has been fortunate to be able to blend his passion with his career. Recognized as a leading presenter in the field of education, his message about the importance of teaching has resonated with hundreds of thousands of educators around the world. Todd is Research Professor at the University of Missouri in Columbia,

Missouri, and Professor Emeritus at Indiana State University in Terre Haute, Indiana. He has spent his life pursuing his love of education by researching and studying effective teachers and principals. Prior to moving into higher education, he was a math teacher and basketball coach in Missouri. Todd then served as a principal at the middle school, junior high, and high school levels. He was also a middle school coordinator in charge of staffing, curriculum, and technology for the opening of new middle schools. One of the nation's leading authorities on staff motivation, teacher leadership, and principal effectiveness, Todd has written 65 books including the national best seller, *What Great Teachers Do Differently*. Other titles include *Your First Year*, *Shifting the Monkey*, *How to Get All Teachers to Become Like the Best Teachers*, *The 10 Minute Inservice*, *What Great Principals Do Differently*, *Motivating & Inspiring Teachers*, and *Dealing with Difficult Parents*. Todd is married to Beth, also a former teacher and principal, who is a faculty member in Educational Leadership at the University of Missouri and Professor Emeritus at Indiana State University. They are the parents of three children: Katherine, Madeline, and Harrison.

Acknowledgments

We would like to thank those who have served as our heroes, while we have worked to provide something relevant to our K–12 superintendents who make a positive difference in school districts every day. A special "thanks" to Superintendents Dr. David Hoffert and Rob Moorhead for their prepublication assistance and expertise with our manuscript, both first and second editions. To our many friends, colleagues, and students at Indiana State University and the University of Missouri, we want you to know that we value your support and the encouragement you provide. Finally, to our wives and families, we send our gratitude and love for the continual inspiration you offer, as we are lucky guys indeed.

Introduction

We wrote the first edition of *The Hero Maker* in 2017 and were overwhelmed with the positive response. Many of you shared ideas you would like to see incorporated into a future publication. We also had many discussions about how school leadership and governance have changed just in the last few years with some of the events that happened and are also currently impacting schools, leaders, and boards of education. Thank you for your kind words and many excellent ideas. They are always greatly appreciated and have helped generate this new introduction, one shared virtually identically—both in this book and in our companion book for boards of education, *The School Board Member's Guidebook*. With such important collaboration and mutual respect necessary among both groups, we felt a consistent introductory launch into the importance of the content that followed was a must. When reading, please know your dedication is truly amazing during all times, especially the most challenging. School leaders really demonstrate what excellent leadership looks like and you should be proud of that every day.

In some ways 2017 was not very long ago, and in others it may seem like an eternity. There have been a multitude of events that have impacted school leaders since. Some of them are local issues that apply to your district or setting only. Others have had a much broader impact. It may seem like the world is upside down, and at times we may wonder if it is all worth it. Let's examine a couple of changes and then weigh how we are dealing with the swirl of contemporary educational leadership.

Covid

The pandemic is one of the first things that comes to mind that was a direct challenge for all school leaders in the years since the first edition was published. This was something new, and there was little in recent history to understand how it should be handled. Unless you were a survivor of the Spanish flu pandemic—and if you were congratulations on living to be over 100—these were uncharted waters. Decisions had to be made that impacted almost all settings, such as moving to virtual learning overnight and when to reopen. A great number of challenges moved us to district-wide virtual learning (the pandemic, then the need to continue to educate, then finding the best way to do so, then to train, assist and enable that to take place across all schools and grade levels, then how to work with students who lacked technology access, etc.). It was hard, and one of the main reasons for this was that we didn't have a dress rehearsal; we went straight to opening night. It is easy to criticize someone else's decision, but it is difficult to make that decision yourself. People always look to leaders, but during times of crisis, they stare. And there have been a lot of staring opportunities since 2017! Additionally, we needed to navigate mask policies for students and adults when we all returned to in-person learning. We are hesitant even to mention the vaccine debate which is still somehow a hot topic in certain places.

Some of these policies were mandated differently in different states and locales. If a governor mandated schools going virtual, the impact on superintendents was more logistical: "How can we do this most appropriately?" rather than the more divisive question, "Should we do it at all?" If we had patrons, employees or board members who didn't agree with the directives, their anger was more likely to be focused on leaders at the state level versus local leadership. This potentially avoided family feuds that might divide the district. Because it was mandated from above, it had more of an "us against the world" rather than a "civil war" impact. People might not agree with the decision, but they realized local leaders were limited in their actions.

This is an excellent example of what can happen when leadership is passed on. If at the federal level we say every state can make their own decision, then pressure is shifted from the country's leaders to the state leaders. If the state leaders say every district can make their own decision, then the pressure is shifted to the local district leaders. This is not a judgment of how things should have been handled. It is rather an understanding of how pressure can seemingly be increased or decreased as we take or avoid responsibility.

Just think if at the district level the board and superintendent said, "Let's let each school decide a mask policy." It is easy to see how that would increase the likelihood of anger at the building level versus the district level. Then, what would happen if every principal said that since the teachers know best, they should decide the masking policy in their own rooms. Now the teachers would be under great pressure for their decision, pressure they wouldn't have had to feel if the decision had been made at a higher level. This example can help us make tough decisions at our own level so that others are not required to make them at their level.

Sadly, many superintendents were caught in this storm because of board members' differing views, or the sharp differences of opinion in their communities. Both sides may have felt they were 100% right, with no way of really knowing what was best. It was a landscape rapidly changing in real time. All this was exacerbated by the social and political divides across seemingly every level of the country—which was the second impetus to write this edition.

Social and Political Divides

Schools have increasingly been in the firing line of many political battles and attacks. In some settings, it feels that more and more schools are being demonized, and sadly at times great rewards are provided to the attack dogs leading the charge. Certain people who have no real knowledge of how schools work seem determined to work very hard to challenge educational practices. This may have been the case in the past, but social media, political shows, TV channels, as well as blogs, podcasts, etc. have fanned the flames.

Historically if an angry parent came to complain to a principal, board member, or district leader, it was about their child and something that happened at school. The family member felt that grading was unfair or a punishment was inappropriate, or their child was not getting enough playing time on the basketball team, for example. We would hope they could behave appropriately with their concern, and we could work to find a reasonable solution. But even if they seemed to be totally out of control, one thing was still holding them back. It was that deep down they knew their child was coming back to school at some point, and they didn't want to completely dissolve the relationship. We could have patience for the most belligerent parents who are complaining because their child is important to them (at least we hope so) and they were trying to be their advocate. They responded personally because it was personal, and both they and you wanted what was best for their child—even if your viewpoints were different. They had a truly caring concern which was why they were so emotional.

However now, because of podcasts, etc., there are people who want to fight schools when they do not even have children in the district. Or, even worse, they don't even live in the district; they just live to fight. The difference between a sincere parent coming in and sharing their concern about language they feel is "inappropriate" for their child, and a person with no connection to the school district printing off a banned book list from the internet and demanding to search the school library because the devil has come to town, is huge. They have no connection, no personal skin in the game, but can use social media to try to rally their troops near and far.

Because of social media and other sources, often the views held aren't even their own personal opinions. They are just sharing the worked-up views of a podcaster or influencer that they follow. They have been told a mysterious enemy is afoot that no one can see, and they are here to root it out. They have a fake solution to a false problem, whether it is a belief that there is kitty litter in the classrooms so that students dressed as "furries" can go to the bathroom in the class, or that kindergarten students get on the school bus in the morning a boy and come home that afternoon a girl, or any other made-up issue. There is no possible solution to a problem that doesn't exist, but it is very hard to prove a negative. School leaders know of course that it is difficult to even give a student an aspirin without family permission, let alone do surgery at school, and if there really was a class with kitty litter in any school, there would be pictures all over the internet and the "news reporter" would be broadcasting outside of the school with their own furry costume on.

Leading your district and school board to put out fires rather than fan the flames is one of the challenges we have always faced. However, it is important that we work to help everyone under our watch understand the truth and correct any misinformation they have shared or failed to refute.

The More Things Change

We might take the view that things seem completely different now, yet actually they are amazingly similar. People say the world is different after Covid, but isn't it reassuring how many teachers are doing their best and making a difference every day? The political noise can be loud, but the impact our schools have on our communities can be even louder. Our job is not to reflect society, it is to cultivate society. We may have some renegade community members—or even board members—but don't you know so many people who are doing the right thing simply because it is the right thing? Never lose sight of the difference schools make. We can all think back to when we were a student and remember our first-grade teacher, our fourth-grade teacher, and our sophomore English teacher. A lot of us can recall our school bus driver or one of the custodians. The children under our watch will remember their educators as well.

Make it a point to visit schools and classrooms regularly just to remind yourself why you have chosen the challenging, amazing, and rewarding task of being a school district leader. Take pride in that. Schools have always mattered, and they always will. Thank you for choosing to help guide and mold the future. Thanks for helping with the hope. What you do matters now more than ever. It is exhausting because it is essential. Thank you for providing the vision, guidance, and support for so many others. That's why you are a leader, a hero maker actually. Thank you.

Addressing the Challenges:

One time I was working with a group of state leaders, and they asked me what to do about all of the classrooms in their state that had kitty litter in their room. I reassured them that no schools in their state had kitty litter for kids to use to relieve themselves. They asked how I could be sure since they hear so many rumors of this. I asked them if any students in their state had cell phones. Of course, their answer was yes. I then asked if any of the students' phones had a camera. Once again, a resounding yes. I then ask them to open their own cell phones and search for pictures of kitty litter in classrooms in their state. Weirdly, there were no pictures. Zero. I shared with them that there are no pictures because there are no classrooms with kitty litter. And their obligation as state leaders was to tell everyone that there are no classes with kitty litter. Additionally, I shared that they should contact anyone they have ever talked to about the issue, because if they didn't refute it when they talked to them the first time, it then became a fact in the mind of the other party. That is the role of leadership. At every level.—*Todd*

And Acknowledging the Similarities:

As I travel schools in our nation and beyond, I'm reminded of why this is the absolute best time to be in our profession—because it has *always been the best time* to be in education. One reason has to do with the enduring qualities allowing us to thrive in our role. Admittedly, some of these come more naturally to some, yet most can be taught to anyone here for the right reasons.

This is evident in my daughter, who as of the writing of this book is currently preparing to be a teacher. Much of what makes her successful revolves around the same skillsets I used 30 years ago and continue to use to this day—these include a way of thinking about things, and a way of doing things. So yes, things might be different nowadays, as we hear all the time, but the big similarity is that success with new things is really much the same as it always has been with new things. And we're equipped for this success, if we leverage our leadership to define new circumstances as opportunities.—*Ryan*

1

The Hero Maker

The relationship between a school board and the superintendent is fascinating and complex. The superintendent is typically chosen and hired by a school board and then answers to this same leadership body. This seems simple enough. We get hired by a group and then also must follow its leadership and expectations. Most jobs fall under this type of structure. However, many factors make the dynamic between the superintendent and the school board much more complicated.

A board is not one person, which we can picture as a traditional "boss." Instead, it is a group of individuals who may or may not function together in a healthy or professional fashion. In addition, it may be a group whose membership is composed of changing people. A new superintendent might be selected unanimously by a five-member board and just months later, three new "bosses" are in place because an election resulted in a 60% turnover of the board. And these three new members may have a completely different vision of what they want their superintendent to accomplish. Their

> **A board is not one person, which we can picture as a traditional "boss." Instead, it is a group of individuals who may or may not function together in a healthy or professional fashion.**

vision may not just differ from that of the three members they replaced; it may also differ dramatically from that of the two existing members and from that of the other recently elected officials. This, in and of itself, is an incredible challenge. But amazingly, this may be the easy part.

What is unique is that superintendents must then have the skills and abilities to lead their bosses. This delicate balance makes the superintendent–board relationship so complex. A trained and educated professional such as yourself must lead an organization under the guidance and supervision of people who potentially have little or no training or education in how to govern your organization. And simultaneously, they decide your fate. The quandary is that if you allow the board to tell you what to do, you may not be doing what is best for the organization, yet if the board isn't allowed to exercise its elected authority, their public may not be getting what it wants, nor the representation provided for them under the law. Compounding this situation is the fact that as policymaking power has been taken from local communities, boards are often left focusing on more ground-level issues, which get in the way of your leadership. If superintendents cannot solve this complex puzzle, it becomes almost impossible for them to be effective in promoting school success and leading the principals and teachers under their guidance. This book is designed to assist with this tightrope walk.

Diversity in the Ranks

School board members may have incredibly varied backgrounds. Some may be former teachers, principals, or even previous superintendents. Within this group there can be past successful educators who get the "big picture" and work to help advance the district to do what is best for all students and staff. Also, within this group may be someone who was fired by the school board at a previous time and who potentially has a desire to hold the current members, and even you, as their personal target bull's-eye for criticism or job sabotage. Shooting at this target is this person's biggest incentive to become a district governing board member.

Some school board members have successful businesses, farms, or professional practices, while others have nothing else to do. There may be individuals with five children currently enrolled in the district and others with zero. They can be volunteers or receive a significant stipend for their roles. There can be board members who have a district-wide perspective and others who have the goal of getting their nieces jobs as teachers. One member may be a lover of sports, and another may want the football coach fired because his son is not the starting running back. One may feel that the cheer team should have additional funding for new uniforms, and others may have the view that the spirit squad should be disbanded.

There may be members of the group who have advanced degrees and others who only graduated from the school of hard knocks. Some may have a wealth of common sense, and others may seem to have a dearth of it. Put all these different perspectives together, and it can seem overwhelming. But the next challenge may be even more daunting. With no positional power over the board, the superintendent must be able to teach and influence these individuals to function together to make decisions based on what is best for the students and school district. Being able to do this with no formal positional advantage is a task that at times can seem challenging and even overwhelming. How is it possible to lead our bosses? Should we even attempt it? Are there more effective ways to do so?

Are There Any Commonalities?

Upon first reflection, it may seem an insurmountable task to *lead* this group of individuals down a common path when they may potentially have such dramatically differing backgrounds and viewpoints. It can be difficult even to conceive of how to meld them into any type of cohesive group. Sometimes just getting them to "play nice" in public can be a challenge. Is there anything that we can do to influence those who are our employers, when we are the employee who is required to answer to them? How can we help them successfully sort through the many voices they hear from the public: From the club, in the shop, and/or around the neighborhood?

We know why you might, at times, have a tight feeling in the pit of your stomach. Yet, we believe that you will be successful in this incredibly important position, despite the seemingly no-win playing field. You will do this by discovering some things that we all agree on.

Although it may seem that a group such as your board of education has such different members that it can't have a common ground, there *is* one thing these members share. All school board members want to make a difference for their groups of constituents. Or to put it another way, each member wants to be a hero. That's right, a hero. And your job is to help them accomplish this in a positive and productive fashion.

All school board members want to make a difference for their groups of constituents. Or to put it another way, each member wants to be a hero.

The board member who runs for the position to cut taxes, the member who has a goal of getting rid of the girls' basketball coach, and the member who wants to help pass a referendum or bond to build a new school, all have one shared outcome: They want to be heroes.

Now, you may be thinking that some of these viewpoints would make them lots of enemies or would lead to harmful results. You may be correct. These members may have the minority viewpoint or may have an aim that common sense tells us would lead to more harm than good. But in their minds, if they accomplish what they set out to do, the result is they will be heroes to someone who matters to them.

One may feel like her daughter will be so proud of her if mom can get on the school board and get rid of the basketball coach who cut her "baby girl" from the squad in her sophomore year. Others may interact with a political group that wants to cut taxes, and if they can help make this happen, they will then be supported to run for a more significant office in the community. An individual could hope to be elected or appointed to the board so that funds can be raised to build a new high school that will positively impact future students and the community for generations to come. Although in some ways their goals may seem contradictory, the underlying aim is to be held in a more positive regard by others.

> **Although in some ways their goals may seem contradictory, the underlying aim is to be held in a more positive regard by others.**

For some members, these "others" might just be the people sitting around the dinner table in their dining room. Some board members might see the benefit of providing a better education for students and how that can assist the community through a more educated population. And some members might seem to have a visible agenda, yet there is a chance they are not even aware of what their actions are suggesting to others around them. This could be true even if they profess their purpose is to serve all students, or even if they don't really know why they are on the Board. In that regard, they have a blind spot and can really become their own worst enemy, from a reputation standpoint.

Making Heroes

One task a superintendent must focus on is how to position these individual board members as heroes by helping them do the right thing instead of something else influenced by their own personal agendas, especially if their individual agendas may not be what is best for the students and the district. When we can accomplish this, we can then help those who are our supervisors come together in a more cohesive way to realize their goals of being heroes.

One of the primary purposes of this book is to help district leaders understand the importance of hero making. A second and potentially more challenging aim is to help teach and develop the specific skills needed to accomplish this daunting task. To do this, we discuss in the chapters ahead the constituencies that influence board members and fuel their desires to be heroes. We talk about boards of education and their responsibilities in our system of education. Since the superintendent's role is critical to the success of the board, we talk about how superintendents serve as a

Shield for boards, so they are protected when making the right decisions. We also discuss how the best board meetings are conducted, and what the superintendent should do between meetings so that school leadership functions well. Finally, we discuss the individual board members with whom superintendents come into contact, and how they are motivated to make decisions, no matter the communities in which they serve. We even show how superintendents can start undefeated each year—and for those who are considering a new challenge, we pose the question, "Is there a time to move on?"

If you are a district leader, you are highly aware of the incredible responsibility you have. Every day, your actions and decisions influence hundreds, or even thousands, of young people in your schools. You knew this responsibility when you chose your leadership role. You wanted to make a difference. Now we must figure out how to make an impact, through the making of heroes. Your students deserve it. The final goal of this book is to help school leaders understand that making others into heroes accomplishes the same result for themselves. A true hero is someone who helps others accomplish things they didn't think were possible.

A true hero is someone who helps others accomplish things they didn't think were possible.

Thanks for what you do. Thanks for making a difference. Every day.

⭐ Hero-Making Tips

- Hero makers make an honest appraisal and ask themselves: "What characteristics and behaviors do I have that influence those with authority over me to want to be led and taught by me?"
- Hero makers then ask that same question of someone who will tell them the truth.

- Hero makers strive internally to "forgive others (meaning board members) in advance" for how they approach the board–superintendent relationship initially, as prior experiences in their lives have potentially trained them to be disagreeable or even hostile.
- Hero makers ensure that board members can look backward with pride and forward with hope, when approaching official roles or envisioning acting on an issue.
- Hero makers realize something shared with us recently by a friend of ours who is a superintendent: "There are two kinds of community members: board members and future board members." Each community member whom superintendents meet could someday be their boss, and hero makers act accordingly.

2

Constituencies

A superintendent must keep an eye to the sky, much like an air traffic controller, with radar scanning to ensure the right planes are landing at the right times, on the right runways, and at the right airports. We don't want people crashing into each other. The pilots are more aptly described as powerbrokers in any given community whose job it is to carry passengers (those whom they serve) from one destination to another, typically from a place of "needing something" to a place of "getting something." The passengers associated with each powerbroker make up the constituencies, or groups, that influence the life of any superintendent.

Understanding Expectations

Each constituency has expectations.

We might have the Music Boosters constituency in one group, the Chamber of Commerce in another, and the Teacher's Union in a third. What is fascinating about these constituencies is that in most cases, each one has a cause they believe in, and taken separately, most of their causes by and large make sense.

Think about it way: What's wrong with putting more resources into music? What's wrong with running schools more like a business, in terms of how dollars are spent and costs contained? What's wrong with giving teachers a raise for the hard work that they do? Nothing really, if these issues or actions are taken separately. But these groups do not see the full picture. When groups become so ingrained that the only view they see or hear is a view like their own, it becomes challenging to expand their way of thinking.

Social media compounds this situation.

We would think that having access to the views of thousands of others could help us all learn and grow. Of course, it could—*if* we were to interact with and appreciate those who have differing viewpoints. However, if we only associate with like-minded people online or otherwise, not only do we believe we are correct, but we may also think that there isn't even another point of view at all.

This is not to indict social media. It is an important tool; however, it does help to be aware of how board members and other constituencies who only interact with those who share the same views can have trouble seeing alternatives to their world. And believe us, these constituencies will be quick to point out what their world is all about, with no clue of its limitations. Their quick, negative comments provide an imbalanced view of any given situation.

As stewards of the community dollar, superintendents have only so many resources to go around and investing in one constituency typically brings an obligation to de-invest in another, unless you are going to spend money you don't have. Over time, these investment decisions have a tendency to alienate people if not handled delicately, especially when everyone thinks their "baby" is the cutest (and that by not paying special attention to it, you're calling it ugly).

Embracing Complication

With constituencies, things can get complicated.

To try to list all constituencies a superintendent needs to handle (and what to do about them) would be counterproductive, because communities are all different. We can say, however, that anywhere you go, you will find several constituencies, and their motives will invariably contradict one another. Superintendents who do not forecast this never-ending state of contradiction are probably a bit naïve in the job search. The saving grace is that what *is* common in all communities is the fact there really is order within chaos. Constituencies do have predictability. Because of this, superintendents have a great resource from which to establish focus and priority.

All they must do is to study their boards of education.

After all, individual board members are often elected upon the shoulders of constituencies who feel most compelled to turn feelings into action. They are often elevated to office by those who feel most strongly about issues affecting their children or community, and thus make great informational conduits that superintendents can use to gather information, and then prioritize decision making. Superintendents must at times filter information that board members bring to them, as some board members are only in tune with the perspectives of their group, yet even fringe information is valuable.

When meeting together, the board of education becomes its own living "constituency," as members (ideally) coalesce and paint a clear picture of community sentiment. Boards of education become their own poster children of what should be "urgent" in a superintendent's life, and what should be "important."

Constituencies, Uncovered

As does any constituency, the board of education has the following characteristics:

1 It has issues that define it.
2 It has power and influence.
3 It has people.
4 It can behave irrationally.

Yet, more importantly:

5 It has a hierarchy of needs.
6 It wants to be a hero.

Think of the local group that wants to start a new academic tutoring program in your community, and they want it funded with tax dollars that currently go to your school. On the surface, one may hear them talk about issues of "family choice," "equity of opportunity," or a host of other issues that can define the group's agenda. It is hard to argue with any of these issues because the underlying values seem to make sense. Of course, we would like to think we are already providing good tutoring to students, and maybe we are, but that's not the point.

A constituency is out there that feels differently.

The group might also have power or influence, which might include the backing of several prominent community members. At times, you might see some irrational behavior, such as zealotry or public criticism of you, with some scud missiles fired. Many constituencies might possibly have a few crazies they keep around, to create helpful distractions for their own greater good.

Yet, what this group could also have, for sure, are needs.

The group and its membership have a need to be heard, and some of the individual members probably have not been heard in a long time, or at the minimum they feel they haven't, which is just as relevant. They might have a need for peace at the dinner table or breakfast nook, and each day for the past ten years they have been fighting with their children to go to school. Maybe they have a need to keep the promise they made to their children that school will eventually get more tolerable for them, and currently they are unaware how to ask for help. Maybe they are unobservant and don't realize your local school is already providing wonderful tutoring (and pays for transportation to and from), yet what is really going on is that they have a need to be thought of as smart, in the eyes of their own children, for the first time in a long time.

Maybe they have a need to take a few shots at the principal, not because the principal is ineffective, but because they had an ineffective principal who they did not like 20 years ago and 100 miles away, and it is time to right the wrong they lived. Behavior such as this is quite often related to personal experience in school.

Now these things might be 100% not your school district's fault, but they are felt viscerally, in terms of someone's needs, nevertheless. Often a person's experiences feel so personal because they are so personal. If you feel something strongly, it can seem that everyone else must have the same emotions. These underlie the professed issue of tutoring. The constituency has a need, too. It has a need *to meet the needs* of its membership. In short, it needs to be a hero. Beneath the veneer, all groups (and many individuals) are like fragile adolescents when it comes to their basic needs. Superintendents who understand that are in the best position to make a difference.

> Beneath the veneer, all groups are like fragile adolescents when it comes to their basic needs. Superintendents who understand that are in the best position to make a difference.

How Hero Makers Handle Them

Our best superintendents help promote the positive energy of constituencies, rather than working against their bad energy. They pay more (and positive) attention to those issues that are mutually agreeable among constituencies, and they provide less attention to those that cannibalize others' agendas. One might even say that hero-making superintendents help constituencies to exercise their good legs, and don't pay as much attention to the rehabilitating of the bad.

If the Boy Scouts and the local tobacco lobby share a common interest in helping the local humane society build a dog park, it will be the conversation topic around the campfire, and in the cigar shop too, most of the time. It is not so much a matter of "what" the superintendent pays positive attention to, it is "that" the superintendent is paying attention to something important to the constituency. Attention really is quantifiable (continually tallied, by the public), as is positive affirmation during those times together.

Paying attention and providing positive affirmation are really opportunities to treat people and their constituencies like heroes.

Our best superintendents work with constituencies by starting with the "hero" (from the constituency characteristics previously noted), forgiving in advance any irrationality they encounter, and moving into addressing the real needs people have—which some people aren't even aware of. Knowing that constituencies want to be heroes to those they represent, and board members want to be heroes to those constituencies, allows superintendents to meet the groups' needs for safety, love, and belonging. Once these needs are met, the board becomes much more pliable, as do the constituencies, and are much less prone to dysfunction. Over time, through a superintendent's guidance and caretaking, these constituencies enhance their own power and influence to address positively the issues that are important to the constituency in the first place.

Smart superintendents can establish common ground so their own issues, needs, and goals seem congruent with those of their constituencies, even when they are very different. They start with understanding and finding the need to be a hero in everyone, particularly in those on their boards, then moving through needs, to get to the people inside.

Smart superintendents can establish common ground so that their own issues, needs, and goals seem congruent with those of their constituencies, even when they are very different.

Where this is particularly important is in the public recognition by the superintendent of the issues important to constituencies each year. We don't recommend that this is done through a town hall meeting with the expressed purpose stated and advertised. That would be like inviting a bunch of hungry cannibals to a buffet dinner. Instead, deft hero makers realize the opportunity lies within school improvement and strategic planning processes. These annual planning and improvement meetings serve as an incredible opportunity to bring constituencies together for a conversation, and more importantly, for needs-fulfillment (although never advertised as such), all the while improving schools along the way.

School Improvement-as-Constituency Leverage

Hero makers understand school principals are the boots on the ground of any successful school improvement initiative. Yet, superintendents play a pivotal role in the overall coordination and strategic planning for school improvement assignments and activities district-wide. Consider the following: Critical to school improvement processes is to have a careful selection process of those members of certain constituencies that will attend. Hero makers realize that they need strong constituency representatives who are respected and connected within those groups, even among the more fringe members of the group. Yet they do not want the more extreme members, of course, or those insecure or too weak to serve as an ambassador when reporting back to the group on how the school is giving consideration to the group's agenda.

In the best school improvement processes involving constituencies, the hero maker remains a traffic director, and like an air-traffic controller, understands that others can best pilot. Through the conversations that take place regarding how the school is doing and what it can be doing better, the hero maker asks key constituents to work alongside educators to make the school a better place. Equally important, by asking everyone in the room what issues are important to them with respect to education in the community, the hero maker is showing these people they are important and valuable. A natural outgrowth are key assignments for members of certain committees, yet with the committee chairing best left to the educators.

Again, the school improvement process or strategic planning in any school district is certainly undertaken for the expressed purpose of improving one's schools; this is a must-have and the bottom line. However, these processes in any school district can serve as a leverage point for meeting the needs of constituencies so that hero makers can actively work to ensure others' needs are met, and thus bring out the best in constituencies and the people in them.

Hero Making Exists at All Levels

Although we are focusing on how board members all want to be heroes, never lose sight of the fact that so does everyone else. The movie *It's a Wonderful Life* resonates as a classic for lots of reasons, but one of them is that we all want to be important, remembered, and significant. In some part of everyone's heart is the desire to be "the biggest man in town." Who hasn't dreamed of being George Bailey at some point? We all dreamed when we were younger of scoring the winning basket, being the lead in the play, or nailing the dismount from the uneven parallel bars.

Our dreams may have changed, but they have not disappeared. Maybe it is catching that big fish, nailing a long putt in your Saturday golf scramble, or having your child say, "You are the best in the world"—whatever it is, it still resides in each of us.

District leaders must also work to invite everyone to feel significant and encourage each employee to feel special. As our skills develop, we can then apply them to new and more challenging situations. If we do not have the desire or ability to invite those we supervise to feel like heroes, we will probably not be able to invite those we work for to feel that way. By practicing these skills consistently, we are much more likely to have them become a part of our repertoire. By teaching those we supervise how to practice them as well, these approaches can help spread warmth in our district. We need to find ways to teach our school building leaders (principals, directors, etc.) these same skills so that they can ensure the faculties and staff in their care feel valued and important on a consistent basis.

If we do not have the desire or ability to invite those we supervise to feel like heroes, we will probably not be able to invite those we work for to feel that way.

Not only do we need to model this behavior, but we must also intentionally develop these same skills in everyone who serves in a leadership role. Once infused throughout the building level, principals can then help bring these same practices to the classrooms so that teachers can invite every student to feel like a hero. As we build these skills in our district, it makes the next referendum we need to take to the voters in the

Inviting others to feel like they are special helps them work harder and develop a much higher level of loyalty to our students, our schools, and ourselves.

community seem less daunting. Inviting others to feel like they are special helps them work harder and develop a much higher level of loyalty to our students, our schools, and ourselves.

> ✪ **Hero-Making Tips**
>
> ♦ Hero makers ensure that as "air-traffic" controllers, they don't fly the plane. Their job is more about giving clear air space to others who have the controls.
> ♦ Hero makers understand the best practical use of air-traffic controlling is to listen more and talk less; facilitate more and direct less; and remain above and outside the direct, play-by-play interchanges between building leaders and constituency representatives.
> ♦ Hero makers recognize and accept that those who comprise a board member's constituency are those who comprise a board member's constituency. Those close to your board are "a given." Hero making is not akin to parenting, where we try to get our children to make *better friends*. With very few exceptions, this would not work out well with constituencies.
> ♦ Hero makers keep their eyes to the horizon for the next constituency that has an itch that is not getting scratched, because the board is not yet paying attention to it. This may be best done in coffee shops, the car mechanic's waiting room, the dental chair, or the barber shop/hair-styling salon. This is a prime opportunity to teach a board member to reach out and connect positively.
> ♦ Hero makers ensure that board members are a part of school improvement efforts, but don't necessarily assign them to the same committees with constituency representatives with whom they may have unhealthy relationships.

3
The Board of Education

Boards of education typically have plenary power (total power) to conduct the school's business locally. One problem is that in many cases, they operationalize their authority in ways that go beyond what an optimal working relationship would provide. This chapter presents a model that works, one that hero making would help to foster.

Under ideal circumstances, the board of education has four main jobs: (1) hire and fire the superintendent, (2) set policy, (3) act on the budget, and (4) represent community sentiment. Beyond these, our best boards get out of the way and let superintendents do what they do best—lead. Other boards see the need to get their fingers into places they don't belong, whether through micromanagement or throwing their titles around individually.

We do concede that superintendents and school boards do, from time to time, exercise overlap of roles and responsibilities. Noted authors Bradley V. Balch and Michael T. Adamson (2018) list desirable skills common to both, including affirming mission, building substantive school–community relations, and tolerating ambiguity, among others. Where we depart with these authors is the notion that both entities (board and superintendent) must "lead a complex educational organization" (p. 2), as well as their mention of "considerable overlap" regarding roles and responsibilities. Here's why we depart. First, we believe leading is ideally handled by leadership and only leadership, not those in governance wanting to be the leader; and second, if there's much overlap, that doesn't mean it's good overlap. The authors do make an excellent point that each (boards and superintendents) understanding *what* the other is charged to do, as well as transparent communication, is critical for amicable relations.

Superintendents tell us it is hard to address issues of micromanagement, because board members sometimes take offense at critical conversations that arise because of it. We don't believe there is any upside to addressing these circumstances *through the front door* with direct conversation having to do with something board members "should stop doing." After all, underlying a board member's nose getting stuck into the school's daily operations is a need (psychological or otherwise) that is not currently being met. Addressing the behavior without addressing the underlying need is just silly and, at best, a temporary solution.

One need of the board member is, as we have mentioned, to be a hero—possibly to keep a promise made to someone or an obligation felt to the core of one's existence. How can we compete with that? Well, we cannot, without getting on the same side as the board member—not on the side of their micromanagement, but on the side of scratching their itch, so to speak.

Meeting a person's need is not that complicated but requires finesse and a genuine desire to understand that person, to bring about a conversion regarding the behavior we want instead.

How Optimal Working Relationships Happen

The optimal working relationship between boards of education and superintendents starts ideally as soon as the superintendent is hired or maybe even during the interview, because this is where the superintendent has typically one "win" (the job) and no "losses" (the job). It may be the last time you feel undefeated, so milk it while you can!

Yet it can start anytime, really. It just gets harder to establish the longer the relationship is not at the beginning optimal starting point.

One main strategy is necessary to fostering positivity: Make time to reach out and stay connected to board members individually, as often as they need reassurances that their voices are heard loud and clear. Whether this is a morning coffee at their workplace, a lunch "on the superintendent" (not the district), or on the sidelines of a soccer field, it is critical for superintendents to prioritize this time with board members individually.

During these meetings, if the board member is talking much more than the superintendent, the visit is doing what the visit is supposed to do. It is critical for the superintendent to casually mention what the optimal relationship would be, without talking about an optimal relationship. The more you listen to someone, the smarter they think you are. Here is an example:

> **Make time to reach out and stay connected to board members individually, as often as they need reassurances that their voices are heard loud and clear.**

> You know, Cathy, one of the things that I always keep in mind is not to veer from the policy decisions you and the board make. Once you all provide guardrails for how we operate, I make it my mission to handle the details for you. You can count on me. I always appreciate your taking the time to share your concerns, as it allows me to better understand what's important.

Another example:

> Hey, the one thing that I can assure you, Bob, is that I know who my boss is—seven great people who get together once a month. Whatever you vote on that night, whether policy, budget, or even my contract, you can rest assured I'll take care of the details. The last thing you need on your plate is ground-level stuff.

A Delicate Lesson to Learn

One important point that board members probably should learn, *through the side door*, is that they only really have the authority to do what they do when they meet as a group. Individually, they do not have official authority to do anything. Their only voice is the entire choir. They cannot come into your buildings and direct your principals around; they cannot give teachers orders or tell coaches who is going to start on the basketball team.

Okay, we realize some of you may be saying, "They sure can!" And you are right, when things *aren't* right, they run around doing some of these things. We bet there are a lot of you out there who have found yourself in proximity to board members behaving in this fashion.

The point is that board members really *should not*, since most often under the law they do not have the power. Hero makers understand how to get this behavior under control, without having to quote song and verse of state statute. In ideal circumstances, the board will somehow learn these things through the professional development opportunities you provide them or through informational materials your statewide school board association shares, or even better through the casual conversations you have with them as you prioritize your time, one-on-one.

As an aside—one thing we will discuss later in the book is that when a superintendent organizes a professional development experience for board members, the superintendent should always attend as a learner themself. Rather than nod or point out a board member's faux pas when the outsider provides direction, we can and should *be a peer* and act like it is *new knowledge* for us to learn as well. Rather than giving the impression we knew something they did not, it may be better to help everyone feel that we are all learning simultaneously. This can prevent insecurities from arising, which can dampen building a collaborative relationship. Sometimes the best leadership comes when people feel you are below them or at least on a level plane.

Using language such as, "Someone suggested that we might…" or "The other day I heard an idea…" can be much more palatable and can build collaborative relationships much more than "Do you know something I thought of…" or "I think we should…" Taking the approach that we are all learning at the same time and making everything be someone else's idea can lower the guard or defensiveness at key times.

Noted again, a model that works is when boards of education hire the superintendent, set the policy, authorize a budget, share community sentiment, and then let the superintendent lead. And yes, an occasional whisper about what this group wants, or what the group is worried about, is helpful for board members to relay, though much-better shared with the superintendent in a coffee shop at 7 am than through grandstanding at a board meeting.

There is nothing worse than when every board member wants their remarks entered into their own personal Congressional Record during a board meeting, especially when the newspaper reporters stop by or members themselves are preening for the live stream being shared. That only perpetuates a model of governance and leadership that does not work, because rather than listening, too many are just awaiting a pause in the jabbering to interject what they want to say.

I'm Just Looking Out for You

Helping board members do the right thing, because it is in *their* best interest, is an essential element to the training process. As we've said, it's important to share with boards, from the beginning of your tenure or the beginning of their tenure as new board members, how they should not have to spend their valuable time dealing with ground-level details.

For example, if board members receive a call from an upset parent, they should not have to take their valuable time trying to resolve it. Feel free to encourage board members to have the parent call you directly so that they do not have their evening spoiled by a purportedly urgent concern someone tries to drop in their lap. And then make yourself available to field the call, which is an important caveat. When you get the call, you

> **Helping board members do the right thing, because it is in *their* best interest, is an essential element to the training process.**

can redirect it to the appropriate building leader, after providing a listening ear.

Now, what if it is something the board members want to be a part of—if it is something they feel will make them a hero if they can resolve it? Help them understand that although this time it may be something they are interested in—i.e., the football team coach selection (pet project for a specific board member, let's say)—they really don't want to deal with it because the next call might be about the pompon squad try-outs, wrestling or basketball gym practice priority, or National Honor Society inductions, and they might not want to get caught up there!

Help them understand whatever ground-level action they take (or how low they go on the organizational food chain) to solve or address an issue, this action becomes the standard for which they will have to address all issues. In other words, if they decide to try to have a three-day suspension overturned, no school administrator will want to make decisions at that level in the future because it might be overturned and result in a public embarrassment for the school-level leader.

In addition, the school board has now sent a message to the community that if they do not like a building-level decision that involves a three-day suspension or any similar kind of discipline, they can just bring it to the board's attention, and the board will "fix" it for them. Help them understand while doing it this one time may move them up temporarily on someone's hero meter, it runs the risk of forcing them to make potentially unpopular decisions on a regular basis, which will have the opposite long-term result.

Although this time they may feel heroic, help them foresee what can be forthcoming because of this decision. Reassure them you value their input privately, but the parents who complained are better served when they understand it was not the board member who made the final decision.

Also, teach the board member that when hearing parental or community complaints, even any personal commentary or an eye roll can put them in a bad situation in the future. Saying things like, "We'll take care of this for you!" when a parent shares a story can be all the spark needed to set off a powder keg of fireworks in the future. Hero makers teach their board members that once they get down and wrestle in the mud, they will be expected to do so time and again, and sooner or later, they will want to opt out of the match, and this will be awkward for them.

Although we mention it would put the board member in a bad situation in the future, it obviously puts superintendents in an equally bad or worse situation. We know this. However, we also know that some board members may or may not care if they cause you future struggles, but for sure they do not have any interest in adding to their own personal grief down the road.

> **Hero makers teach their board members that once they get down and wrestle in the mud, they will be expected to do so time and again, and sooner or later, they will want to opt out of the match, and this will be awkward for them.**

That is why hero makers plant these seeds with their boards. It pays to remind them that if they as board members mishandle an issue even once, those same board members will potentially be the ones to deal with the anger and unhappiness as future decisions mount. We want to keep them off this trajectory. And we want them to appreciate that from us. As hero makers, if we do not start with teaching our superiors, we will find ourselves in situations where we have all the responsibility and none of the corresponding authority, and this is an incredibly stressful dynamic from which to try to lead.

Synergistic Relationships in Leadership and Governance

Before we close this chapter, we should mention the need for synergistic relationships in leadership and governance, as depicted in *Minds Unleashed: How Principals Can Lead the Right-Brained Way* (Donlan & Gruenert, 2016). Applied to hero making, it is when three important entities function well: The superintendent, the board, and the board president. If these three are doing their jobs optimally, things typically go well in terms of school governance and leadership.

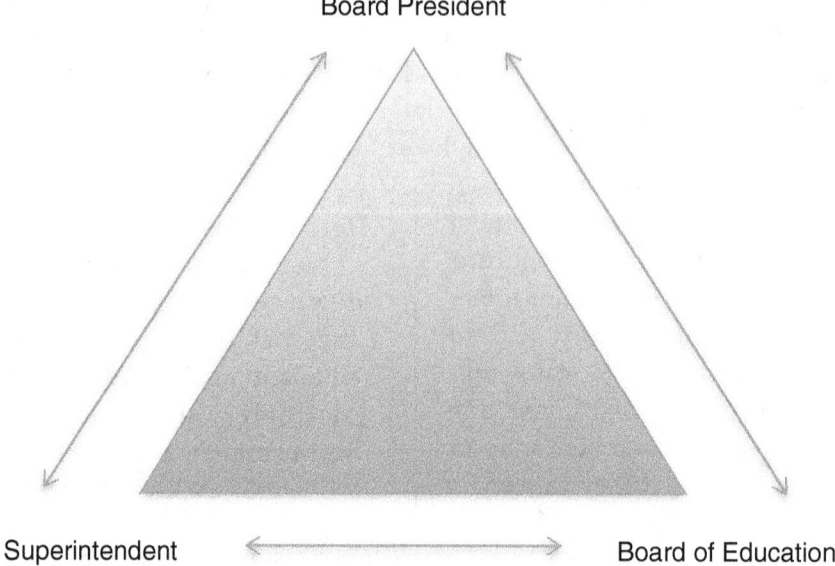

FIGURE 3.1 The Relationship Between the Hero Maker, Board of Education, and School Board President for Optimal Governance and School Success

Source: Adapted from Donlan and Gruenert (2016) to the notion of Hero Making.

Again, the board's role is what we have described in this chapter (policy, budget, etc.) as the "what"; the superintendent's (leading and managing) is more the "how." The board president has a special role in that he or she helps the other two groups establish four components necessary for a good relationship: Trust, deference, assurance, and humility (Donlan & Gruenert, 2016).

Trust. Superintendents must trust that their boards represent accurately what their communities want from their schools; boards must trust superintendents to handle the details. Boards must trust that their board president and superintendent communicate often enough (ideally weekly) (Donlan & Gruenert, 2016). When boards feel like heroes, trust is easier to maintain.

Deference. Boards must be willing to defer day-to-day operations to superintendents; superintendents must defer to boards when policies need to be made (Donlan & Gruenert, 2016). Both boards and superintendents best defer the operational details of the schools to their building principals, and instructional decisions to the teachers and staff. Consider how much easier it is for a hero to show appropriate deference than it is for a non-hero.

Assurance. Board presidents should give assurances to superintendents that their day-to-day authority will not be questioned. Superintendents should provide assurances to board presidents that weekly updates will occur. Board members would ideally provide assurances they will not intentionally micromanage school operations (Donlan & Gruenert, 2016). We contend that boards who feel like heroes have the confidence to provide assurances.

Humility. Everyone together must realize with humility that mutual support is the key to a positive relationship (Donlan & Gruenert, 2016). As hero making allows for confidence building, boards can better demonstrate humility.

Ideal Board Governance and Who Should Attend Board Meetings

Board governance—or its process of making decisions toward better outcomes for the school district—ideally starts with board members who realize the power and opportunity in their staying above the fray (operations). It allows them the opportunity *not* to feel they must provide kneejerk assurances to their hardware-store customers or to the patients in their practices who render complaints.

In fact, a board spending time on ground-level action (the sprint) is actually abrogating its responsibility to quality governance (the marathon). This reminds us of the sage wisdom we received when we were young and were ascending the educational food chain, regarding how much time educators have to make a decision. Teachers are bound to respond to something in the moment. Assistant principals sometimes have the luxury of a bit more investigation. Principals can schedule

> **A board spending time on ground-level action (the sprint) is actually abrogating its responsibility to quality governance (the marathon).**

a meeting to prepare a decision on most things, and superintendents can wait a bit longer, because they may want to gauge how different constituencies will react.

Board members, in terms of their governance, have the luxury of sharing with constituents that they would be happy to bring up their concerns at the next board work session. Doing so might make a good percentage of the angst go away naturally, if mindful follow-up accompanies it. It also allows board members to focus more on the larger issues that superintendents rely on them for:

- policy changes that may affect the district for the next decade
- school safety decisions influenced by pressing concerns yet finite resources
- curricular adoptions that could make a powerful difference in the skills children take with them into higher education
- staffing decisions that may be with the school for the next 30 years
- approval of purchases that enable moving the school district mission toward vision
- community sentiment, in terms of infrastructure and support for facilities
- statutory developments that may influence how policies are prioritized and resources utilized

These issues are the stratospheric issues that must be thought through deliberately, prudently, and deeply by some great minds indeed. Although it seems that at times pedestrians win elections, hero makers are effective at allowing board members to realize the large import placed on their time and talent. If they are kept focused on handling the heavyweight issues, these will take their time and energy, so it behooves the hero maker to help board members understand *who* must handle *what* work, and on behalf of whom.

Further Items to Ponder, Regarding the Board of Education

Boards of education, when fulfilling their roles publicly, oftentimes will require additional information beyond that available. The temptation does exist for superintendents to have on hand a gaggle of gainfully employed central-office and building-level administrators to provide an information-sharing service to the board, as decisions are being weighed. We urge caution here. Quick answers are often not the best answers for your board, and putting your team on the spot does not help them out. The undue stress in preparing for monthly events (i.e., public board meetings) that invariably will expose your folks to criticism will detract from their peak performance you expect daily, and from their trust in you as well.

Consider as well that the differences in time span available for making decisions as we move up the food chain is one reason we need to think if we want board meetings to include members of building leadership, such as principals and assistant principals. Although it makes for a nice way to have building reports reach the board, having the building administrators present during community remarks can be a bit more tenuous. Potshots can be taken. This can be awkward for members of the board, whom we are trying to keep as heroes. Boards may feel obligated to request immediate responses for accusations tossed. They may even be tempted to act more quickly than they should... if at all! This puts good people on the line, without much time to deflect, and it can even get legally complicated.

If your administrative team is typically on hand for board reports, having building administrators excused from the venue by the time community remarks are offered can go a long way toward defusing issues. In this way, the board president or superintendent can then say to any aggrieved party, "This will be looked into by the principal." If building leaders must be present, because that is simply what the community expects and boards are unwilling to budge, it pays to coach your building administrators not to offer any committal answers at a public board meeting, but rather to acknowledge the concerns and offer to meet privately with the concerned party to fully discuss the issue.

We understand there may be times when the superintendent wishes the transportation director, head of maintenance, or principal were at a meeting to answer a question from a board member or provide information in response to a public inquiry. However, there may be times that the superintendent is glad they are not there, so that a time lapse can be used to our benefit to gather information and prepare an appropriate and consistent response.

We find weaker superintendents may too often allow their leadership team to get attacked verbally at board meetings, so they themselves are insulated. Hero makers certainly do not do that, because this is not what effective leaders do. They are aware that in all situations they are ultimately responsible and work to protect their employees by keeping them off the front lines whenever possible. Superintendents and their teams have enough daily responsibility and pressure. There is no reason to increase this at a public hearing. Plus, if our building leaders do not provide an immediate and satisfactory response, there may be more damage control needed than we might wish. Additionally since the majority of board meetings are live streamed, an individual situation that would not have been shared publicly if the principal were not in the meeting, is now being discussed throughout the community before there is ample time to investigate conscientiously and address it.

Hero makers know when a community member shares a complaint or concern during the open forum, asking that person to contact you tomorrow can be a way to sift out how important it is to them. If your phone is ringing at 8 am the next morning, it must really matter to that person. If you never hear from them again, this may also indicate how pressing it was. This does not mean that you do not follow up; rather, it may help to frame the essential nature of their issue. As with many negative people, some of your community members can jump from issue to issue so quickly that if you can put off a response for even a few hours or days, they have moved on to something else.

★ Hero-Making Tips

- Hero makers clearly articulate an optimal board–superintendent relationship at their job interview in terms of the four clear roles of the board (the "what"), and leadership expectations of the superintendent (the "how"). They then look closely for the board's reaction, without appearing to do so, to gauge agreement on good governance, and whether they want the job.

- Hero makers newly hired might well be cautious in situations where board members justify direct involvement in operations, by saying they are only doing so because of a void left by the previous school administration. Beware if they say things will return to normal, *after a while*. If the situation prior to your arrival really was so serious that board members are "playing superintendent" (and for argument's sake, let's say it was), the speed with which they hand you back your "keys to leadership city" is directly proportional to their confidence in you. If it's not immediate, they are less than 100% confident in you, so keep that in mind.
- Hero makers master the facial expressions, tones, and gestures that are needed to have critical conversations with boards on the advantages they can accrue from not making promises or making knee-jerk reactions when angry people call them. They can convey sincere worry for the board members, almost whispering in their ear convincingly about the problems that meddling will cause them personally, and how they "have their back" in handling things another way.
- Hero makers protect their leadership team from potshots at board meetings by ensuring they are one step removed from public scud missiles and board-level inquisitions. In most cases, this involves not having them attend board meetings and sharing with the board this is your leadership preference. This protects all parties and helps boards in their role as heroes.

References

Balch, B. V., & Adamson, M. T. (2018). *Building great school board–superintendent teams: A systematic approach to balancing roles and responsibilities*. Solution Tree Press.

Donlan, R., & Gruenert, S. (2016). *Minds unleashed: How principals can lead the right-brained way*. Rowman & Littlefield Education.

4

The Superintendent as the Shield

In terms of election or appointment to a school board, board members *put themselves out there* in a sense, in a way that exposes them to critique and consternation. Friends, neighbors, clients, and customers all see them in a new role. And it seems everyone who has gone to school believes they are experts at knowing how schools should be run. Restaurants and schools have a lot in common. We have all been in them, so we all think we can run them ourselves. That is probably one reason that the most common kind of business to open is a restaurant. The fact that it is not nearly as easy to run a restaurant or lead a school as we might envision is probably the reason that the most common kind of business to close is also a restaurant.

Non-educators thinking they know how to run a school is as odd as a non-plumber thinking they are an expert in plumbing just because they used the restroom this morning. Yet that is what we deal with constantly, and that is why board members need a hero maker's protection.

We would like to introduce a few metaphors in leadership

> **Non-educators thinking they know how to run a school is as odd as a non-plumber thinking they are an expert in plumbing just because they used the restroom this morning. Yet that is what we deal with constantly.**

and governance that involve bows, arrows, quivers, and shields. It seems like everyone nowadays is carrying around their bows, arrows, and quivers—ready to shoot at school officials. Critical to our awareness, however, should be the public's readiness to shoot at our board members as well. Oh, and even in cases where they are not planning to shoot, we really should want our board members to think that they are ready to do so.

Here's why.

You as a superintendent hero maker are *the Shield*.

And we want our board members to *believe this*!

A healthy bit of uncertainty may keep board members on their better behavior.

Think about a situation in which a board member comes to us, demanding we hire their new son-in-law as the coach of our basketball team, or something similar. In this fictitious case, we actually haven't fired the current coach yet, but the board member is certainly going to be demanding we do this at the next board meeting. They might even mention they've been passing around a petition for others to sign.

Well, you and I know the actual thing going on is that the board member probably has some personal or family dynamics that are influencing them. There may even be factors they don't want aired in public to do with the situation.

The board member would rather make an issue of something that is probably not the real story than disclose their ulterior motive, which is personal in nature. In these situations, the hero maker would be the one to help the board member.

Time for your cape and superpowers—enter the Shield.

In a private meeting prior to the board meeting, and in a one-on-one conversation with the transgressing board member, you'll find a few things work, and they work every time if done well:

First, thank the board member for their efforts, affirm their positive intention, and be sure you articulate clearly what you understand they are proposing or planning. Ask if you are correct.

Next request they share what they immediately hope will result from their planned action, and what higher-level or longer-term goals they hope to accomplish.

Share with them you wish to help them reach a desired result in a way that is going to affirm their perspective, assuage their concerns, and protect them and the school district from criticism or consequences.

Offer you must act initially to maintain respect and dignity for all involved, most certainly board members, as the community will have a "morning after" reaction to any decision made.

Clarify your role as superintendent is often to navigate "when" things happen that bring about a desired result, as much as "what" things happen to do so.

Present clear facts to support your preference for "your own" short-term solution, both viable and logical. This includes suggesting an alternative action to what your board member wants to occur, or even taking no action immediately other than to investigate further (always good).

If you perceive conflict between you and the board member over viable next steps, consider utilizing a technique that leverages the positive energy of critical conversations and conflict, the ORPO technique, from Dr. Nate Regier and Next Element Consulting.

We first learned of ORPO in conversation with Dr. Regier and from his book, *Conflict Without Casualties: A Field Guide for Leading with Compassionate Accountability* (2017). While we do not profess to be experts, we have found success with techniques gleaned from Dr. Regier's and Next Element's discoveries and consider them powerful in hero making.

ORPO involves offering a succession of short statements said in a specific order—the first as we have learned demonstrating our openness (O) or healthy vulnerability in conversation, the second showing our resourcefulness (R) in problem-solving while also paying homage to your board member's capabilities, the third establishing persistence (P) with healthy boundaries toward resolution, and the final, openness (O) once again to check in with your board member.

This process can be repeated and might sound like this:

> [Board member's name], I feel apprehensive where we're going here but hopeful (Open, showing healthy vulnerability). We've explored this situation initially to address

your helpful concerns, and I think we have the capability to learn more and leave no stones unturned (Resourceful, honoring capabilities). I will need a bit more time to investigate and ask that at this evening's board meeting we maintain consistent messaging that things are moving forward productively and will conclude responsibly (Persistence, establishing boundaries). How are you with that (Open, gauging feelings)?

Then after your ORPO statement, you would reaffirm again that, no matter what, you'll strive to be the board's Shield. Depending on what the board member responds, ORPO can be done again, fine-tuned with an attempt to reach consensus on next steps.

Key here is that you are working to protect this board member from themselves; you are their Shield. You are always their Shield, even when you disagree. Know that and embrace that.

ORPO is a great framework for how you use your role as a Shield, verbally, in conversation. It is informational and disarming, and maintains dignity in difficult dialogue. As you continue your ORPO dialogue, be sure you make note that quick action would not be in their best interest. Then, no matter what happens next with their own behavior in public, you can rest well knowing you've done your best on their behalf.

In rare instances, your Shield is disregarded, and that's ok. They'll learn from natural consequences, and things may become uncomfortable for everyone. It doesn't mean you stop providing. It doesn't mean you stop leading and defer.

One other tip may be to always be aware of physical spacing. One technique that can be quite effective is sidling up (Whitaker, 2015) to the person you are communicating with. When there is a connection, people feel that standing side by side can build trust. During times of possible conflict standing next to someone in that same fashion can be discomforting to the aggressor. If we instead stand (or sit) face to face, it actually can empower the person who desires confrontation because that is a natural aggressive stance. Thinking through the dynamics of standing, sitting, or other arrangements can often assist in building trust or disarming someone who might be inappropriately aggressive.

The challenge is continually educating and reminding the board that we must have consistency in how we operate. It is counter-intuitive to choose to go

The challenge is continually educating and reminding the board that we must have consistency in how we operate.

renegade in certain cases, when we want some semblance of consistency in how district administrators handle the situation next time. Reminding board members how important and valuable they are as visionary leaders can help elevate them above dealing with things that will eventually lead to dysfunction for the school district.

✪ Hero-Making Tips

- Hero makers work actively to manage positive relationships at all levels of their organization and community so people tell them things in confidence. That way, they know what arrows might be launched against their board members, or what should be mentioned to their board members as possibilities, so they can then emerge as the Shield.
- Hero makers recognize when board members are unknowingly shooting arrows at their own backsides. The challenge becomes having critical conversations with those same board members as they are shooting arrows—which can have a boomerang effect and loop around to come back at them. Envision yourself standing aside the board member, having a civil conversation, while your arm with your shield covers their backside.
- Hero makers do not run frantically from board member to board member with little shields each time they are about to receive some arrows. The trick is to use shields judiciously to leverage the more important outcomes that you wish to achieve, not simply to handle every bit of "incoming" that seems urgent at the time. Sometimes board members need to feel the sting of an arrow or two to know they don't like the experience.

References

Regier, N. (2017). *Conflict without casualties: A field guide for leading with compassionate accountability.* Berrett-Koehler Publishers.

Whitaker, T. (2015). *Dealing with difficult teachers* (3rd ed.). Routledge.

5

The Care and Feeding of Board Members

Superintendents are in a unique position in that they are employed by boards of education to lead all aspects of school district operations, yet in a strange way, they also act as an educational parent to the board itself. This dynamic occurs because the superintendent is the one who has been schooled in the trade knowledge associated with running an educational institution, and the board might not have been. Some board members may be clueless about the demands of contemporary school districts, with their only expertise being the fact that they made it through the 12th grade themselves.

Thus, much like a child's first teacher is their parent, a board member's first teacher is ideally the school superintendent. This is odd, in that board members are offering them a contract and writing the superintendent's pay check, yet it is still a fact. And just as in parent–child relationships, the burden of the responsibility of the care and feeding of children rests with the parent; in this case it is the superintendent who is responsible for the care and feeding of their board.

Hero-making superintendents do this exceptionally well… most of all, by *not* overthinking it.

Care

Superintendents provide for the care of their boards very simply by ensuring their lower-level needs are met before encouraging that their higher-level needs be met. We've all learned about this need hierarchy which comes from Abraham Maslow, an American psychologist. Maslow's theory denotes that a hierarchy of needs exists in all of us, and before our higher-order needs can be met, our lower-order needs must be satisfied. The first needs are physiological, then involve safety and security, and then have to do

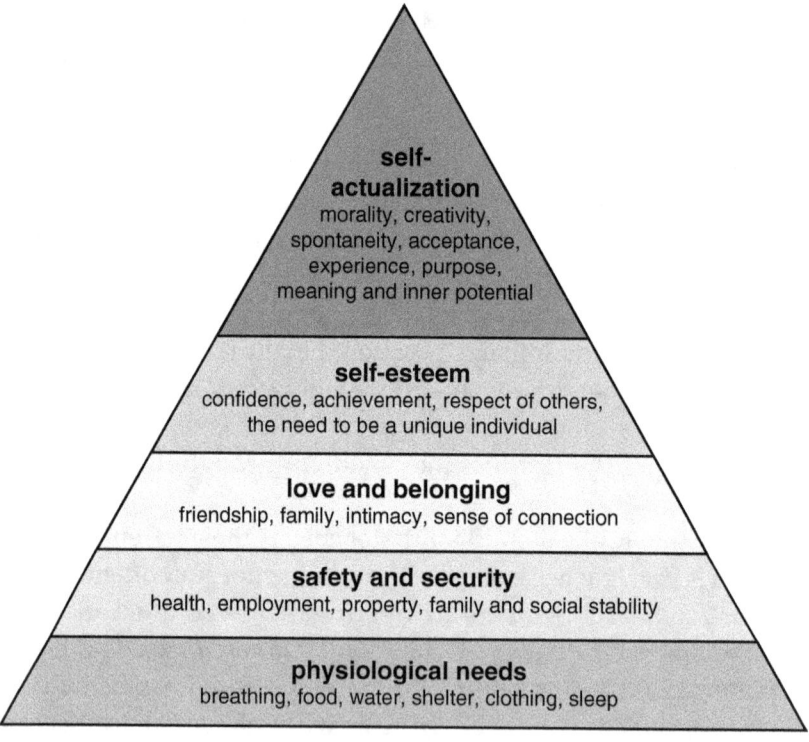

FIGURE 5.1 Visual Depiction of Abraham Maslow's Hierarchy of Needs

Source: Originally published in Maslow (1943).

with belonging and love, then self-esteem, toward eventual and hopeful self-actualization. A visual of this hierarchy is shown in Figure 5.1.

We understand new layers of needs have been added to Maslow's model in recent years (such as cognitive needs, aesthetic needs, and transcendence needs), yet for simplicity's sake, Maslow's original pyramid will suffice.

Physiologically—and with respect to safety and security needs—hero makers ensure at every juncture, board members' service and the decisions they make are going to be safe for their livelihoods and families. As we noted, superintendents serve as Shields, by protecting board members from public criticism and discontent. Imagine if the superintendent allowed for a partnership of the school district with a new-to-town, big-box retailer, in a way that would put the local hardware store owner/board member out of business. Or imagine if the superintendent steered the board in a direction that was so unpopular that local folks boycotted board members' businesses. That would not do any good for the care of any board member.

Hero makers do not lead their boards astray. They know what is both "safe" and "unsafe" for their board members and work toward doing what is right by the children of the school district, at the same time protecting their board members while doing it. They need to anticipate what is going to cause a problem for individual board members, even if those board members do not anticipate the problem themselves or dismiss it.

That is just what hero makers do.

Feeding

Not ignoring other areas just as critical, hero makers who are effective with their boards are often working in overdrive to feed the board members in Maslow's areas of love, belonging, and self-esteem.

Hero makers who are effective with their boards are often working in overdrive to feed the board members in Maslow's areas of love, belonging, and self-esteem.

Nearly all board members are on boards for these two reasons, which makes sense to us in that folks who feel like heroes are, by definition, loved and belong, with self-esteem a natural byproduct.

Hero Makers and Love and Belonging

Areas for love and belonging include those of friendship, family, and a sense of connection. Hero makers know how important these are to board members and work to create situations in which board members feel like they matter, both professionally and personally.

Board members who feel "loved" see their picture when they walk into the district's schools. They feel loved when receptionists know who they are and refer to them by name. They feel loved when they are constantly introduced in public as selfless individuals who are the real keys to the many positives that are happening in the district.

Hero makers ensure board members' photographs are visible on websites and publications present in school offices, waiting rooms, and on hallway tables. Board members feel loved when they get cards, paintings, and drawings from students. Board members feel loved when the basketball team brings them autographed schedule posters to hang in their dens or home offices. Hero makers ensure they work with principals so there is a planned, yet quiet, rotation of care packages that come to all board members from children at strategic times of the year.

Yes, hero makers orchestrate expressions of love.

Board members "belong" when they arrive at a board meeting and are greeted warmly by the superintendent and secretary. They belong when smiling faces make conversation with them prior to the call to order—principals, teachers, staff, and others in attendance. Board members belong when the superintendent knows enough about them and their interests, so that principals and teachers send invitations to them for classroom visits and special events. One board member might feel very much at home in the music room; another might love to tour the culinary arts or building trades programs. Board members experience belonging when hero makers know enough about them to know what makes them feel right at home.

Yes, hero makers orchestrate belonging.

Hero Makers and Self-Esteem

Hero makers are intentional in fostering self-esteem in board members during meetings, through what they say, how they come across, what they do, and how they organize things.

Areas of self-esteem include confidence, achievement, respect from others, and the need to be valued as a unique individual. Hero makers know how important these needs are for their boards. They strategically plan to mention board members at certain times during each monthly meeting's agenda. They ensure board members hear about other board members' accomplishments during discussions so that each member can look backward with pride and forward with hope, as Robert Frost once wrote (though admittedly, not about school boards). Being affirmed in front of others builds self-esteem.

Board members also experience a boost in self-esteem when superintendents echo and contextualize their remarks during board discussions. The last thing board members want is to make a point, then have the discussion abruptly move in a different direction. When this happens, they don't feel heard, and they can be embarrassed. Hero makers serve as *human transitional phrases* to ensure smooth segues in conversation when some people just need to be quiet for a while, maybe saying things such as:

> And you know, Angela does make an excellent point in that one of our goals should be to ensure that the junior varsity parents are just as able to see their children's competitions from their bleachers as the varsity parents... and that is why it is particularly important that we hear from Robert, who shares that concern but wishes to note something that we as a group may need to consider as well.

An interesting byproduct that we believe has a bit to do with the self-esteem of a board member is that of self-efficacy.

Self-efficacy is the belief that we can make a positive impact through hard work and earned effort. Self-efficacy is critical for positive board leadership and sound governance. Board members who have self-efficacy tend not to be insecure—not to delve quickly into conspiracy theories or rant about the haves and the have-nots at board meetings or on social media. They tend to stay away from playing the victim, and from helicoptering and rescuing. With self-efficacy, board members have a healthy sense of personal and professional autonomy, and rather than bring about more problems they tend to roll up their sleeves—whether in conversation or action—and do the critical work of governance. Hero makers know that the path toward fostering self-efficacy may come through self-esteem, in that one might need to feel good about oneself before believing one can set goals, execute strategies, and make things happen.

> **Hero makers know that the path toward fostering self-efficacy may come through self-esteem, in that one might need to feel good about oneself before believing one can set goals, execute strategies, and make things happen.**

So, what does all this psychological stuff have to do with good governance?

It has a critical place, really, in terms of the board's readiness and continued energy for its governance role, because governance is tough! It involves continually learning to operate as a good board member at a 30,000-foot level, where the best (or worst) decisions can have a lasting impact for decades, all the while resisting the temptation for short-term fixes that will play well in public.

It involves being receptive to new learning, while one whom you are supervising is serving as your teacher. That's a unique relationship, one which relies on the notion of "Teaching Up."

"Teaching Up," Alongside Care and Feeding

Teaching Up comes from the notion that teaching does not need to end whenever school leadership begins (Donlan, n.d.), and this is true for any level of leadership, including the superintendency. It is critical in leadership.

Consider that any leader teaches up, down, and around daily. A hero maker certainly does.

Teaching Up means hero makers teach things to those who are their superiors; Teaching Down means hero makers teach things to those who report to them; and Teaching Around means hero makers teach things to those with lateral relationships. For superintendents, this could mean the board of education (up), everyone employed (down), and community partners, such as the chamber of commerce president or a non-profit CEO (around).

The care and feeding of a hero maker's board involves Teaching Up, as Figure 5.2 notes.

Hero makers who Teach Up have a role as a *confidant* to their boards. They *safeguard* each board member and the board as "Shields," as we presented earlier. Because in many cases superintendents have professional credentials, occupational wisdom, and educational experience, they *supplement* the board's talents in helping to navigate school district issues and provide for good executive-level decision making. And as loyal employees, hired by and reporting directly to the board, they *serve* the governing body's best interests in carrying out policy, executing a sound budget, and acting in the community's best interest.

So how does this all fit in to care and feeding? Once lower-level needs for care and feeding are taken care of for the board

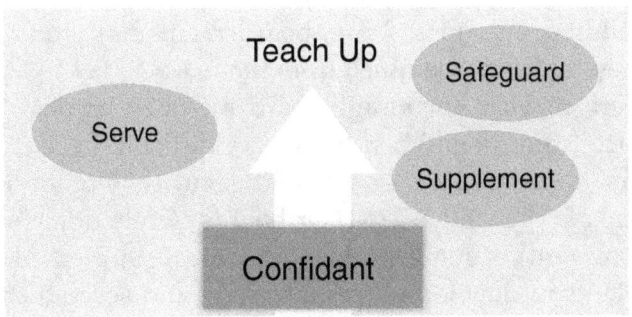

FIGURE 5.2 Hero Makers Influence through "Teaching Up," Including Their Role as Confidant and Noted Responsibilities

by hero makers, then responsibilities as a confidant, such as safeguarding, supplementing, and serving, are better received, if this makes sense.

Hero makers also teach the entire district administrative team to thank, acknowledge, and build the importance of school board members. Through a trickle-down effect, effective building leaders help their faculty and staff members do the same. Not only does this assist with board relations, but it also teaches others to build effective relations in all aspects of leadership. Superintendents also help administrators learn that issues and concerns are not to be directed to board members but rather to the appropriate district-level leader. This may seem like something that should inherently be known, and it probably should be, but if we do not help teach and educate our own employees about proper protocol, we may find ourselves wishing that we had!

Board members are no different from the rest of us, and over the course of our lives, we have all experienced the need to be cared for and fed. This continues in perpetuity for everyone, if we are honest.

⭐ Hero-Making Tips

- ♦ Hero makers strike a balance in relationships with board members. Like good parents, they do not want to be too standoffish or the relationship doesn't flourish, yet they do not want to be too much of a friend either, in that their children (i.e., in a sense, board members) won't think they can learn too much from them.
- ♦ Hero makers encourage board members to seek guidance from them when things get difficult, because they can be trusted for safety and security. Our best hero makers "Teach Up" to their boards (while doing so as a confidant), safeguard their priorities, supplement their talents in developing perspectives, and serve their best interests if aligned with the best interests of children and families.

- Hero makers know how to have discussions with board members that do not mention "them" (board members), but really are about them. This has to do with having their back. Instead of mentioning how the consequences of a particular board action could adversely affect a particular board member's business or family, a hero maker would use a circumstance that is similar, or an "Imagine if..." so that the board member can make this extrapolation for himself or herself.
- Hero makers frame discussions and critical conversations so that board members feel any intended angst privately on the inside (and then go home that evening thinking about it discreetly).
- Hero makers use numbers to their advantage and ensure that others in their school district know how to provide care and feeding as well. Many hands make for lighter work, and when feeding is occurring at all levels, the less the superintendent must do individually. Why would one want to be seen running around the dinner table pouring everyone a glass of milk, when the milk can be passed around?
- Hero makers, through their actions, show board members how to provide for the care and feeding of other board members, and at times for themselves.

References

Donlan, R. (n.d.). Conceptual illustration developed by co-author Ryan Donlan.

Maslow, A. (1943). A theory of human motivation. *Psychological Review, 50*(4), 370–396.

6
Board Meetings

Board meetings are meetings held by the policymakers and budget-setters of the school district to conduct the board's business. They are not town hall meetings. They are not intended to be meetings where the board micromanages aspects of school operations better left to its managers and leadership team. Rather, they are meetings where a group of duly elected community representatives come together to provide governance—thoughts, perspectives, guidance, and oversight—on whether or not the school is operating within the guidelines established by policy, whether the budget is being spent wisely, and whether or not the superintendent is doing their job as chief executive/operating officer.

It is a lesser-known fact that board meetings are the only time board members have legitimate governing authority under many state statutes. When a quorum is held, as per the board's bylaws or state law, the board can then act to conduct business. This is much different than the perception by some that board members, any time they wish, can show up in school buildings, park their vehicles where they wish, tell principals what to do, and show up in teachers' classrooms to see what is going on. In those instances, board members are community members, just like anyone else, and if community members cannot do it, board members should not be doing it either.

We may assume that all board members know this, but realistically how could they? Part of our responsibility as hero makers is to teach them what is appropriate. Training from state or regional school board associations or outside consultants can be used to provide these lines of demarcation to the board as well.

We recall instances where seemingly board members who specialize in operating as a "free agent" have visited the buildings of some of our colleagues and tried to intentionally stir up trouble. One story we heard was where a board member tried to get teachers to fill out a "Petition of No Confidence for the Superintendent." Another concerned a board member showing up in the wood shop to use a tool for a home renovation project. Yet another noted a board member who loved to accompany the drug dogs through the lockers, not realizing they really didn't have the right to conduct a search.

Board meetings are important in ensuring that the best decisions are made, that the best practices of discussion and deliberation are followed, and especially that every board member leaves the building feeling better than before they arrived.

The point here is that board of education meetings are the only *real* time board members have actual authority, and they occur either once a month, twice a month, or quarterly in more rare instances. Therefore, board meetings are important in ensuring that the best decisions are made, that the best practices of discussion and deliberation are followed, and especially that every board member leaves the building feeling better than before they arrived. They also need to operate appropriately because much of the time they have an audience watching who might want to pull out the "gotcha" card at a later date.

You might have guessed it. The superintendent's job is to ensure each board member who walks out of a board meeting feels like a hero.

Here is what hero makers do to ensure that each board meeting goes better than the last one.

Creature Comforts

During board meetings, is the environment inviting? Are the parking lots plowed and the walks swept? Is someone cheerful (possibly a student) standing at the entrance of the administration building or school to greet board members as they arrive? Do board members see pictures of themselves at the entranceway, almost as if they were present members of a country club or even better… past presidents? Does the place *smell* inviting?

If the meeting is held in a school, do board members see custodians still mopping the hallways near where the board meets or if the garbage is still being emptied, bags sitting in the hallway? We hope not. If this is still going on, someone is probably not doing a proactive job in advanced preparation, and *that someone is the superintendent* (because the principal is not doing theirs). *Things roll uphill, of course.* It is critical to have an impeccable, inviting walkway, from each board member's vehicle all the way to the board member's seat at the board table. And then back again.

Are food and drinks prepared? Not necessarily one paid for by the school district, but a small, inviting snack, a modest meal perhaps, prepared by the superintendent or others willing to do it voluntarily. Homemade soups are a nice touch, as are hors d'oeuvres and finger foods. You don't want something too sloppy, but something just enough to tide-over your board members if they have come directly from work and did not have time to stop for a bite to eat.

How about coffee and tea—decaf and regular? Small bottles of water are nice, or even a glass pitcher of water infused with cucumber, lemon, or orange. You probably know what the favorites of each of your board members are so this can be a nice touch.

Are board members seated in comfortable chairs, in a place where they are comfortable sitting? Do board members have respectfully stylish nameplates in front of where they sit so that the public visiting can know who they are (but more importantly, so that each member can feel valued by having a nameplate)? Does the arrangement of the board table and chairs allow for conversation? In other words, do the outside tables angle slightly inward, so that board members can communicate not only with each other but also with the public?

As a hero maker, your positioning is key. You want to be able to gauge the perceptions of each board member during the meeting from where you are sitting. We recommend you sit alongside the board president, so that you can whisper something in their ear if needed.

Is adequate space and positioning provided so that board members can stand up, sit down, and stand up again, and are they able to refill beverages or appetizer plates without disrupting other board members or getting between the board table and the public? It might be nice to allow board members a special grazing area that is unobtrusive to navigate.

Finally, do you have someone positioned and on-hand to tend to any needs board members might have? For example, there might be a need for technological assistance, or an additional photocopy, possibly an extra pen or highlighter, or a refill on beverages.

If you do, it might go a long way in meeting board members' needs.

Often, board members will leave a meeting not necessarily remembering everything that was said—but they will certainly remember if their needs were provided for, and how they felt.

Board members will leave a meeting not necessarily remembering everything that was said—but they will certainly remember if their needs were provided for, and how they felt.

Hero makers proactively tend to the ambiance and setting and ensure all is optimal, including everything that is within eyesight or earshot from the time board members step out of their car to the time they step back in it.

Is the arrangement of which board members are seated next to one other, or not, cleverly conceived and designed? Have you ever been at a meeting where a small (we hope) faction or group of naysayers felt more comfortable because they had the emotional support of proximity? Although this may not be something you can quickly change, you can consider it as new members join or different officers are elected.

Climate

Hero-making superintendents are all about relationships of positive, unconditional regard at board meetings. Their *tasks* are done (paper shuffling), long before board members arrive—even before the early ones arrive. Superintendents are not conferring with the business manager or HR director in the office, nor are they whispering with the school attorney at the end of the hall. They are also not arriving alongside board members; they are greeting board members, just as principals should be greeting teachers or students in each school every day.

Superintendents are ensuring that someone is asking board members if they can take their coats or get them anything. Hero makers might want to do this themselves. Superintendents also must pay particular attention to whom, and how often, they speak with board members, because if they do not stay mindful of this, they might unintentionally spend more time with their favorites.

A good rule of thumb is to give each board member at least one positive affirmation. It helps the board maintain energy to stay in a policymaking role. After all, those who feel good about themselves where they are (in policymaking, governance, or life), need not go somewhere else to have their needs met negatively (micromanaging). One reason compliments are so powerful is that they are often so rarely given. The more you compliment someone the smarter they likely think you are.

Hero-making superintendents should find every opportunity to ensure board members are comfortable. Hero-making superintendents are "great contextualizers," offering confirmation of the value of board members' contributions, even when the contribution is more bull-headed than breathtaking. As noted previously, hero makers are the segues between the points made, the transitions between the paragraphs, and the grease for the ceremonial machine. The climate that hero makers provide is one where people feel safe sharing what is on their mind, because what is on their mind usually has some value, even if mis-delivered during distress. More on distress is covered later in the book.

> **Hero makers ensure that they are *all about relationships* first, since it is only through positive relationships that tasks can be accomplished effectively.**

Basically, hero makers ensure that they are *all about relationships* first, since it is only through positive relationships that tasks can be accomplished effectively.

Getting Down to Business

Hero makers will not let board members waste each other's time, nor that of the administrative team, staff guests, or community in attendance. Now you might think we're going to launch into a cheerleading chant for Roberts Rules of Order, but we are not. Roberts Rules of Order provide some structure for meetings that run the risk of becoming a bit more cumbersome in detailed discussion, but to be honest, if you have less skilled individuals running the meeting—especially without a hero maker in the room—Roberts Rules will not do much, except to create a dysfunctional conversation where someone really nasty competes to prove that they know Roberts Rules better than the rest.

> **Hero makers realize that the "how" of communication works much better than the "what."**

Point of order!!!!!
See what we mean?

Hero makers realize that the "how" of communication works much better than the "what." We have found we can say just about anything to people (some things far-reaching, indeed), when we are more mindful of the "how." It is not so much the words, although certain phrases do help, such as "Would it please the board if the administration team…?" It is much more the non-verbals that allow us to get the business done most effectively.

Structures help as well. One that we recommend when allowed is a consent agenda, where items of more rapid dispatch (and ones that can take up a lot of meaningless banter if there are no guardrails around) can be acted on with one motion. Some of these are items of business that occur month after month, such as approving minutes from the previous meeting, or accepting certain written committee reports that come in regularly or authorizing various expenditures when allowable through this method. It is not uncommon to see ten or more agenda items collapsed into one consent agenda action.

The beauty of a consent agenda is that board members receive these agendas ahead of time for review, and if board members feel that items need to be moved from the consent agenda to the regular agenda, they can make that request. It pays to share copies of all documents (electronic or otherwise) with board members ahead of time so that they can structure their thoughts and ready themselves for discussion. Paperwork should be well-organized and signposted, so that everything is in plain view for board members and easy to locate, and consistent in presentation from month-to-month.

Another tip for hero makers is to get a bit of business done—a healthy amount—before offering members of the community in attendance the time for input. Community input time is often when concerns are brought to the attention of the board, and this can be uncomfortable for board members (some love it, however). Either way, this time runs the risk of taking people away from collaborative conversation, so anything you can do to maximize the number of productive conversations before a bit of contention enters the room is a good thing. That said, don't wait until midnight to have your community input, as that is probably a bit unfair, it brings out the crazies, and it will upset the board member whose aggrieved constituency is in the room.

A good strategy is to offer appropriately timed forums for community input, where people get only a few minutes per person to talk, up until a certain point. The point here is to put right-sized guardrails around this time: Enough so the community feels it has been heard, but not too much so that things run the risk of going too long and detracting from the business that must get done. It is very important to put in these guidelines before they are needed.

If we wait until there is a controversial issue and now they are added it can greatly lower the level of trust.

Also, it always pays to schedule those times when the board must go behind closed doors ("executive session" to discuss disciplinary incidents with students, personnel issues with staff, items of attorney/client privilege, contract negotiations, etc.), near the end of the meeting, so that people are not left uncomfortably stewing in some waiting room or hallway together, or even before the public part of the meeting convenes. One benefit of having the executive session prior to the meeting is that it has an ending time, because we don't want to keep the public waiting. It can always reconvene later if needed.

The structure of board meetings, and how you conduct them, lends itself to good business practices and healthy discussions. Oh, and as we said at the beginning of this chapter—board meetings are meetings to conduct the business of the board. They're not town hall meetings, where anyone with children enrolled in school (or otherwise) can filibuster.

That said, hero makers clarify to the public—and in full view of everyone—that although board presidents may respond to their concerns, they may only thank them for their comments and contributions. Other board members are not obligated to respond to folks who are angry with them (although some will love the back-and-forth), and the board is not required to promise that solutions will come their way for grievances aired.

Hero makers, of course, will offer the assurances that folks are "heard," and that the leadership and administration will do whatever it can to look into [this or that] for the board, and will offer the board president a report on what they find, as soon as it is doable.

Hero makers ensure that after the board meeting closes, board members will drive home with the feeling that the evening spent at school was well worth their time, talent, and contribution. They feel great about their leadership and are proud of what they said, and did, in the meeting.

They feel like heroes.

⭐ Hero-Making Tips

- Hero makers ensure that everything done at a board meeting is choreographed, to every extent possible, under their direction. Yet, at the same time, they do not give that impression to others. They are flexible and are open to changes in the moment, as situations prescribe.
- Hero makers spend the weeks and days prior to board meetings getting everything well-organized and disseminated to their boards. They encourage a relationship with their board so that if individual board members have concerns they wish to express, they inform the board president and superintendent prior to the meeting. The key to a good relationship is that no "surprises" occur during the meeting, even if disagreement is to take place or concerns are to be aired.
- Hero makers ensure they use "invisible time" productively prior to each board meeting. This is when they are in the boardroom by themselves prior to anyone else's arrival (except maybe their administrative assistants or custodians), ensuring that the space is properly arranged, that seating is comfortable, that food and drink are available, and possibly even that soft music is playing so that no one arrives to an awkward silence.
- Hero makers are effective at making good recommendations for board action at board meetings. They don't shy away from this role, and they rarely equivocate unless needing more time for due diligence in investigation. This confidence helps to frame issues constructively and gives board members the security to know that the actionable items have been vetted through the thinking process of the chief executive officer. It is a part of acting as the Shield for board members. Board members are then welcome to move forward the recommendation through to board action, or to take a different path, but at least a professional recommendation is provided to the issues in

front of them. And there's never an "I told you so" that follows, if the board goes against a recommendation and things don't work out.
- Hero makers embrace their responsibility to make sure every word or action of their board is affirmed for its merit and contribution, even if it's not the way things are going to move forward. They are magnanimous in maintaining dignity for all board members who contribute to governance, even if counterproductively.
- Hero makers are great storytellers and do so at board meetings without droning on or going on for too long. They augment positively the message of their board president in conversation with the board or members of the public. Their purpose in storytelling is to ensure that those offering contributions can look backward with pride, and forward with hope. They serve as the deft contextualizers so that everyone's comment—even the thoughtless person's—has a bit of window dressing for public consumption.
- Hero makers ensure they bring the *sizzle*, as well as the *steak*, to board meetings. So, before the board takes up any issue or motion, the superintendent has one or two options *that will work* (or at least will minimize collateral damage) so that the board doesn't appear to be out of options (and thus, appear to be unknowledgeable) in front of the public.
- Hero makers ensure that every good idea is someone else's good idea, especially those of a board member.
- Hero makers ensure that everything that goes right via board action is given to the board as credit, and everything that does not go right is embraced as the superintendent's responsibility. This is a part of their role as the Shield. The buck stops with the hero maker.

7

Between Board Meetings

How many of us have experienced the so-called big day, in whatever form it was, and then let our guard down for a few days (weeks or months) afterward? Examples might include the annual standardized testing window, the school accreditation visit, the final game of an athletic season, or even the final day of school in any given year.

"Whew!" We exhale.

Then, we take a much-needed rest.

Superintendents often feel this way after the big board meeting happening once or twice per month, and they especially feel it if they have working sessions between meetings, because these can be equally invigorating (taxing).

Hero makers know that only a brief exhale is wise.

For it is *between* board meetings seeds are sown for the most positive relations with board members. The hundreds of things that occur between board meetings make board members heroes, or not, and as such, they must become the focus of our savviest superintendents.

> **It is *between* board meetings seeds are sown for the most positive relations with board members.**

We suggest a three-pronged approach to ensure heroes are made, and maintained, between board meetings for the best of results:

First, superintendents must make a personal commitment to reach out and do something for each board member between meetings, something that wouldn't be in a superintendent's contract or job description.

Second, superintendents must intentionally be seen by each board member's constituency (key communicators) doing something that, in a positive manner, feeds the appetite (meets the needs) of each constituency.

> **Superintendents must intentionally be seen by each board member's constituency (key communicators) doing something that, in a positive manner, feeds the appetite (meets the needs) of each constituency.**

Finally, superintendents must schedule some official, personal time with one board member per month, for a check-in and update on their perspective as to the superintendent's connection with the community. This is typically over breakfast, lunch, or dinner—or at the coffee or snack shop.

Let us talk about the first item, a personal commitment to reach out and do something for each board member beyond what is in your job description. It might be to write a thank-you note to the board member's boss at work, who has provided the latitude for your board member to leave early once per month to attend the school board meetings. Noting your board member's outstanding service is a nice touch. It could be to attend the funeral for a board member's extended family member, to offer condolences. It could be to show up at a community event the board member is helping organize, offering volunteer time—Toys for Tots, Highway Clean-Up, or Fill-the-Bus for the Soldiers. It might be to see the board member and family at the ice cream shop after the big game or spelling bee and offer your congratulations and thanks to the family for allowing mom or dad to help you with the school. These actions help in hero making. The point is that hero makers become intentional about knowing what is important to board members, and what they are involved in, so they specifically do something with unconditional positive regard to help board members feel valued and important.

The second is a bit more indirect, yet still intentional. Superintendents who know what board members value know their constituencies. They also know where their constituencies spend their time. It is important that superintendents spend time there too, whether at the barbershop/hair salon, the coffee shop, the private club, or the local delicatessen. Key in terms of hero making is being seen having conversations with others, in a way that provides visible support and assistance for those causes the constituencies champion.

If the conversation in the barber chair becomes one of voicing worry and support for the small business owner because of the impending arrival of the big box discount store, then it pays to have that conversation overheard. If it becomes one of praising the recent medical treatment and rehabilitation services at the local hospital's preventative care outlet (and the board member is part of the hospital administration), then that might be a good move as well. If it becomes one of sharing the telephone number of a local politician who can help the farmers get crop subsidies if the drought gets any worse, that might be well worth getting overheard. The point is not that you are inauthentic or calculatingly chameleon-like; instead, you are finding areas in which you can authentically be seen helping board members' constituencies when your values align. Pencil-in those opportunities.

The final point regarding the importance of between-board-meeting hero making is to schedule a formal time, once a month, with one board member to have a candid conversation about how they perceive the school's business is doing, as well as your ability to connect with the community. Then, remember what is said and work to address any concerns the member might have. The school credit card should not pay for these meals, of course; it is sort of the equivalent of what we all

> **Schedule a formal time, once a month, with one board member to have a candid conversation about how they perceive the school's business is doing.**

used to do in terms of stocking our classrooms with the necessary supplies to teach—we use our own money. Same here. You're investing by stocking your personal toolkit with knowledge that will help you lead—and hero-make. These meetings, no more than an hour or so of your time (at your board member's convenience), will allow you to get at the heart of whether you are a hero maker. If you find you are connecting with the community after a "real" conversation, then be assured your board member is someone's hero who is important to him or her.

If not, you have some more work to do.

One question we hear from time to time is this: I cannot even get my board member to talk to me, let alone go out for a meal. What am I to do? In this instance, either this person is in need of a major personality change (not likely to happen!) or your relationship with them has deteriorated substantially. You're not going to make positive inroads quickly, certainly not with pestering for time together. We suggest instead you then choose someone in your school district whom you trust, who is close to that board member, to have the same type of conversation to garner input. If you follow through, word will get back to your board member of the overture, and your attentiveness.

The main point to remember here is hero makers minimize the "exhale" that happens after the big meeting, and then consider each next day's best work as directly proportional to the next meeting's success.

Hero makers minimize the "exhale" that happens after the big meeting, and then consider each next day's best work as directly proportional to the next meeting's success.

If board members feel valued on a consistent basis, they are less likely to need the spotlight of a board meeting to feel important. By nurturing the relationships with board members and appropriately stroking egos between board meetings, you can diminish their needs to feel important when the lights are shining, and the news reporters are taking notes.

Never lose sight of the power of a well-placed compliment. Every time someone receives a compliment, they think the person giving it is just a little smarter. It needs to be sincere, but it can be quite specific.

We always need to look for the good things in others, even if we need to squint.

> Never lose sight of the power of a well-placed compliment. Every time someone receives a compliment, they think the person giving it is just a little smarter.

⭐ Hero-Making Tips

- Hero makers realize what happens between board meetings is at times even more critical than what happens *at* board meetings. Each board member brings to each meeting the cumulative emotions acquired since the last meeting, whether positive or negative.
- Hero makers are on a continual quest for emotion management. They work best to manage built-up emotion through their own version of formative assessment (love that educator jargon!). Through appropriately timed communication between board meetings, hero makers take stock on how issues are affecting the lives of board members, and reach-out to have a conversation. In other words, they get out in front of emotions, before emotions get out in front of them, and everyone.
- Hero makers realize they can *tell* their board members what they stand for (i.e., what they support and believe) all they want, but this won't do much good alone. Board members need to have hero makers *show* them what they stand for, and if this is through the whisper of someone to whom the board member is connected and respects, all the better.
- Hero makers remember if board members resist overtures to have conversations or spend time with them once or twice per year; the refusal is indicative of a future teachable moment, when the hero maker can make a difference in this person's life.

8

The Superintendent–Board President Relationship

Superintendents have a unique job challenge by design. They are hired by a group of individuals and then have the duty to help guide, coach, and lead their "bosses." And depending on election cycles, the individuals who chose them may be quickly replaced by others with a differing or directly contrasting view.

Someone in a somewhat similar situation is the school board president. Board presidents must perform a balancing act requiring a special relationship with the superintendent while simultaneously maintaining transparency and "equalness" with the rest of the board. They conduct a delicate dance of needing to build a tightly linked relationship to the superintendent in order to be most effective, while simultaneously having no more power than their remaining board peers. And they have to be viewed as a neutral liaison to the superintendent and a neutral colleague to their fellow board members.

It is somewhat like the connection between the most outstanding teachers in a school and the formal building leader. They need to be connected to their colleagues and yet serve as a guide and liaison to the principal. They can never be *perceived* as the principal's pet but may have to *be* the principal's pet.

This chapter is designed to help clarify why this district-level dynamic is challenging and yet essential at the same time—and how it serves as an essential connection between the superintendent and all members of the school board.

We extend on the previous chapter on the hero maker's opportunities between board meetings to highlight the importance of a key ingredient in any successful superintendency, the relationship between the superintendent and the board president. This relationship needs intentional curation and effortful maintenance.

Recall earlier on where we shared an ideal relationship between the superintendent, board president, and school board as a whole, leading hopefully to trust, deference, assurance, and humility. We now focus particularly on superintendent–board president interactions as the true driving force of everything good that happens with the school's leadership team and the board as the governing body. We note in some unique instances, you as superintendent report to more than one board of education, such as in cooperatives (or coops). If you're in that situation, this chapter is for you as well. You'll just need to multiply what we suggest, leveraging your interest and investment accordingly.

Key ingredients in the superintendent–board president relationship include perspective taking, targeting, respecting, connecting, navigating, equipping, consensus building, and befriending. All demand earnest effort by a hero maker, which is difficult but rewarding work. We've learned any meaningful relationship in life that is lasting and mutually beneficial takes effort. Like other big commitments, your relationship with your board president is not a 50/50 thing. Sometimes you need to give 70/30; other times it may feel like you're investing 100%. Yet know that over time and with due attention to the ingredients noted here, you'll see the return on your investment, and so will all who work with you.

Perspective Taking

For optimal superintendent–board president relationships, hero makers must have the perspective that they can work with any board member who becomes board president. Admittedly, they have preferences and may secretly wish for some board members over others, yet they never give anyone that impression. What we've learned with boards is that almost all serve because they care and wish to try. We think nostalgically of the times we have been asked to work with boards of education in the past, and invariably the situation has been painted ahead of time (without our asking) that there are some good folks and villains in the mix. More than a time or two, the superintendent has aligned with the "board majority" and asks us to visit and give the board some professional development regarding their roles, duties, or even behaviors with each other. We often find when we arrive is that, yes, things are complicated, and there are usually one or two board members who are feeling their voices aren't heard. That's why they're behaving a bit more counter-productively.

When we check in on how things are going later on, those board members who are not in the majority typically become the board majority within one or two board elections, because they establish a community following and thereby gain power and authority. In short, they take over, and they're now in charge. And one of them becomes board president, with many of those same habits and chips on their shoulder from their former ostracism by the ousted majority.

Congratulations. They're your new board president.

This then becomes your opportunity to start building that superintendent–board president relationship anew, and you can imagine how much better it is starting from a place where you haven't established a negative relationship or side-taking. You're better off at all times as the magnanimous one who sees value in all. Of utmost importance is that you project this perspective always, even with your current board president who will not last forever in their position. Just like the teacher gossiping (or not) in the teacher's lounge, who then becomes assistant principal in that same building later on, when you are thrust into a new world of perspective taking, it's much easier if you haven't been antagonistic to your newfound reality in your past professional life.

In short, better relationships start with a hero maker embracing that they can work with all, and will value such opportunities, no matter who is board president.

Targeting

For optimal superintendent–board president relationships, hero makers must establish and maintain certain targets regarding leadership/governance interaction. These include the four noted earlier in the book of trust, deference, assurance, and humility. These are the most efficient and effective way of operating to keep everything in your school district moving forward, with everyone focused on student and learning outcomes.

What does this mean?

First, hero makers take the responsibility to *put these targets in the minds' eye* of their board presidents often enough so that board presidents are not only familiar with them, but comfortable with them, and even prefer them as they lead governance.

How do you put these in your board president's mind's eye?

We'll share a few examples.

Hero makers working for better relationships with board presidents reinforce *trust*, speak often about the evidence of trust across the district and throughout the schools having a positive impact on students and what the community expects. Teachers who trust families to provide them information on how their children learn best is one example, and showing how school–home relations have leveled up student opportunity through a feedback loop is another. Most board members want to know their constituents are trusted as their children's best experts. With your help in pointing this out, your board president can then have discussions accordingly in board work sessions and open meetings. Trust is also helpfully articulated with conversations regarding site-based management with principals having the latitude to lead in a way that works for them, and in distinguishing the "what" and "how" of the school district. Board presidents who hear about trust often as a way of doing business, with reinforcement from conversations with superintendents, can then model and reinforce trust among board members as well. It becomes a shared target and part of the leadership/governance value system.

Hero makers working for better relationships with board presidents reinforce *deference*, speak often about their appreciation for the policymaking and budgetary prowess of the board of education, with gratitude for these roadmaps provided to leadership. They also provide an example of how they defer to building-level decision makers, and even to task force recommendations and community stakeholders for certain decisions made. In short, superintendents who model deference walk a high road and don't overtly ask that the board behaves similarly, yet reinforce through indirect messaging that deference works. Hopefully, this will result in your board president issuing a tactful call for deference when board action is being considered, or when aggrieved persons ask the board to fix "this" or "that." Deference then becomes a shared target and part of the leadership/governance value system.

Hero makers working for better relationships with board presidents reinforce *assurance*, speak often to their board presidents about the fact that board members can count on the leadership team—not only to handle the demands of their roles, but also that when things go well in the district, they will provide credit to the board's wisdom and governance allowance. Conversely, when things do not work out well, leadership will take responsibility. We spoke of a superintendent's role as the Shield; this is particularly germane here. Board presidents, with reinforcement from conversations with superintendents, can then model and reinforce assurance to board members that at public board meetings, the president and superintendent will bear the brunt of any public criticism. Board members should not feel compelled to respond, with assurance as a shared target of the leadership/governance value system.

Hero makers working for better relationships with board presidents reinforce *humility*, speak often to their board presidents about their service to the board as a continual learner of what the community wants and needs—and further, that the board of education is a superintendent's best teacher regarding constituents. Superintendents remind board presidents of their deep appreciation for clear policy under which to lead. Hero making involves reminding board presidents they know who their boss is, and that this boss is the collective board when they meet each month. The hope is that by the superintendent modeling humility the board president will follow suit with the collective board as well. Board presidents, with reinforcement from conversations with superintendents, can then model and reinforce humility, as it becomes a shared target and part of the leadership/governance value system.

Hero makers use targeting to remind board presidents where all on the leadership and governance team should be going, and as such, they establish guardrails for civility that serve well to fine tune relationships.

Respecting

For optimal superintendent–board president relationships, hero makers take every opportunity to respect both the person and position of board president. This foundationally means a "no surprises" pact between the two of them, so they are allowed to step into their best selves when handling the larger challenges they confront. And if not between the two of them, certainly the superintendent must offer no surprises to their board president. Respecting also has to do with certain aspects of decorum that happen when the superintendent and board president are in public, or professionally meeting with others. In this, the superintendent has the lion's share of responsibility in saying and doing the proper things (i.e., doing the respecting).

Superintendents should use the term "Mr. President," "Madam President," or other similar honorifics when conversing with the board president in professional settings or around members of the public. They will introduce their board president as "President [Last Name]" in professional settings, including building walk-throughs, and even if others use their first names casually because they know them outside of school.

During official board meetings or in public work sessions, when speaking to other board members regarding the board president, a hero maker speaks in the third person, such as "What our President has asked I accomplish is..." or "President [Last Name] has directed that I..." Granted, things are often more informal if appropriate in private executive sessions of the board, but only if the board president insists. Respect for the position and office requires the superintendent's lead in acknowledging a presidential title.

The same holds true if the board president holds another official honorific in their title, such as "Dr." if appropriately degreed; "Fr." (Father) or "Pastor" if a leader or designee of a particular faith-based organization; "Coach" if they are a community icon long of sports fame; or even "Senator" if they previously served in the Senate. These titles do not replace one's title as "President," however in balancing personal respect with professional office such terms may be preferred by the person holding the president's office.

Hero makers leverage more positive relationships with their board presidents by frontloading respect for their position by ensuring no surprises (and encouraging this to be reciprocated), and defaulting to a more formal style of decorum in official interaction, then moving to levels of informality preferred by the board president in appropriate settings, out of respect for the person.

Connecting

For optimal superintendent–board president relationships, hero makers take a lead on connecting at appropriate and timely junctures, to ensure (as noted earlier) board presidents are never surprised by issues in play or on the horizon. We suggest once per week is a good place to start and see where things go from there, where the board president would expect a call or video conference at or around the same time, with that meeting on the hero maker's calendar.

For good relationships to blossom, these meetings do not have to be overly personal or with contrived interest in each other's lives, because that might not be natural. Getting down to business is rather straightforward, with your sharing that you have a short list of items to make your president aware of and asking politely if they have time for a 10 to 15 minute conversation (we'd suggest, and if it goes longer with wishes from your president, so be it). If a sensitive issue is on the list, be sure to share your ideas on how to handle it, then ensure you provide time for your president's perspective. Ask for their guidance when appropriate, but don't be overly needy. Ask to what degree they wish to be involved and be sure to inquire as to what the board might need or expect in the interim.

Sometimes, your board president may decide that alerting other board members to something occurring is warranted. It is then you ask how they would like this done. Stress that if some others are made aware, all others must be made aware (with few exceptions). Key in all conversations involving your board president is that your board president should be talking, sharing, and asking questions, as much as you. If out of balance, you're not investing in your relationship—unless they specifically share that they need a quick update on something. In any event, strive to talk weekly.

Hero makers working to build the most positive relationships with board presidents realize it is both the quantity and the quality of time spent with them that counts.

Navigating

For optimal superintendent–board president relationships, hero makers understand you're going to have some difficult times if you're doing the hard work of running a school. So, be prepared for you and your board president to navigate some treacherous waters together. This might be where some of the closest relationships are forged. Each of you will see what the other is made of on your toughest days.

As one example, you have an opportunity to become closer to your board president when the two of you are having a conversation with your school attorney. These conversations are billable, so do your homework. If you and your board president are discussing a potentially litigious situation with your attorney, ensure you have some ideas to save billable hours. Your solid grasp will be evident and appreciated by your president, as your leadership depends on how well you can keep your school district out of legal trouble. Your school attorney will commend you on that. All this is presented as a permission slip for you to leverage trying times into a closer partnership.

One important consideration while navigating difficult circumstances with your board president is "How much?" and "When?" to share information with others. What you have shared with each other and what you are experiencing is difficult to carry. It's a burden, and oftentimes, it keeps the two of you up at night. Your relationship demands that you decide how much you want to carry on your own shoulders, and when you wish others to help you out. This includes informing other board members. Key also is to decide who out of the two of you will become the heavy-information providers. Consider part of your utility as the Shield; however, there is a certain strength of presidential stewardship developed when one is relied upon to be the beacon of hope when the situation is urgent or bleak. Weigh the pros and cons of next steps together—that's what hero makers and board presidents consider here as they forge a relationship.

Hero makers establish optimal relationships with their board presidents by navigating the most treacherous waters together, and so build confidence in each other.

Hero makers establish optimal relationships with their board presidents by navigating the most treacherous waters together, and so build confidence in each other.

Equipping

For optimal superintendent–board president relationships, hero makers leverage their influence in Teaching Up, as we shared in Chapter 5, and utilize these opportunities as confidant to their board president to *serve* them as information-provider, to *safeguard* them through skill-development, and to *supplement* their talents through the competencies you bring to the equation. In short, you continually equip your board president for the presidency, in all the position demands. Board presidencies are unique, in that as a "board member" they serve in a governance role, and we have maintained throughout our book that when governance and leadership are in their respective lanes, things work out

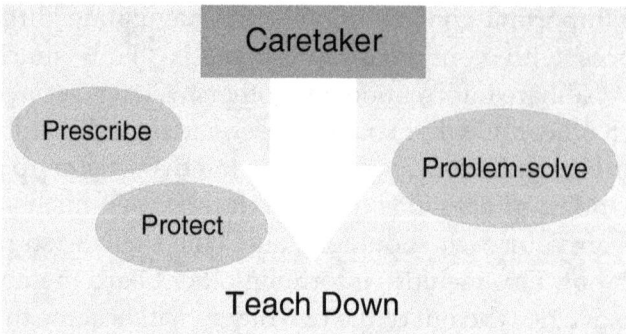

FIGURE 8.1 Hero Makers Teach Up to Help Board Presidents "Teach Down," Including Using Their Presidential Role as Caretakers with Responsibilities Noted

better. Yet, in this case, there needs to be leadership within the governance unit itself, and that is the job of a board president—not only leadership, but management, stewardship, and a certain degree of teaching responsibility to the entire board. We'll now share how your hero-making role in Teaching Up will equip your board president to Teach Down, and Teach Around, and thus to make a difference.

Presented in Figure 8.1 is what we describe as Teaching Down.

Teaching Down (or said differently, downward on the organizational chain) is when those who are higher up in any organization serve as caretakers for others who report to them. Roles in caretaking include prescribing, protecting, and problem solving. Board presidents do all three as they Teach Down.

Board presidents who *prescribe* suggest courses of action for the board to take. They do so after careful consultation with their hero-making superintendents, school attorneys, or resident experts on whatever subject they are considering. Those who *protect* ensure the policies of their boards are in the best interest of their communities and allow school administration the latitude to apply changing circumstances to local contexts. In short, they protect by measuring carefully the potential consequences of actions before taking them. Board presidents who *problem solve* rarely shy away from a governance challenge. They have critical conversations, especially with those who may disagree with them. They weigh the pros and cons of decisions, and then move forward smartly. In Teaching Down, board presidents serve as caretakers for their communities. In Teaching Up, superintendents as hero makers serve, safeguard, and supplement their board presidents to build capacity, so that board presidents are equipped to Teach Down. This is how it works. What goes up, then comes down, as the saying goes. It's an upward investment for the hero makers that will reap dividends in the relationship between the two, as everyone feels better when equipped to do what they're called to do.

Board presidents also Teach Around, and this is primarily to other board members, as we illustrate in Figure 8.2.

Teaching Around has board presidents serving as collaborator, and roles in that regard are modeling, motivating, and managing, as we now describe.

Board presidents who *model* do so in word and deed. They are consummate professionals and see the value in all with whom they work. They are calm and do not get overly emotional. Those who *motivate* can get others to do things they typically wouldn't do by themselves. For the board, this means encouraging fellow members to make tough decisions in full view of their friends and neighbors, oftentimes with limited resources or selecting among groups with competing interests. By motivating those around them who serve, board presidents move everyone to a better place, because if boards are not taking

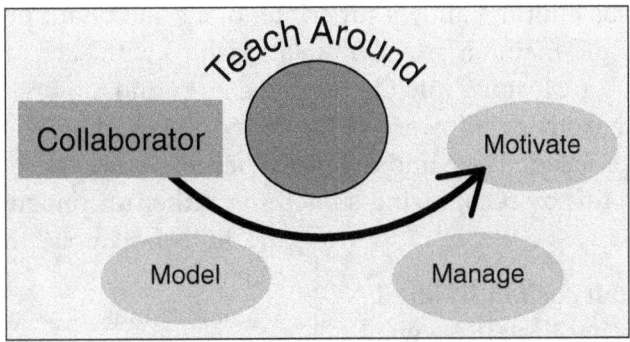

FIGURE 8.2 Hero Makers Teach Up to Help Board Presidents "Teach Around," Including Using Their Presidential Role as Collaborators, with Responsibilities Noted

action on behalf of their constituents even with apprehension of the result, everyone is moving backwards. Board presidents who *manage* handle the operational details of their position with speed, dispatch, and accuracy, so that others do not have their time wasted. Quality management also allows for better decisions, as they can sort and prioritize both information and perspectives, as our best managers know they must do the best with what they have. In Teaching Up, superintendents as hero makers serve, safeguard, and supplement their board presidents to build capacity in their Teaching Around, so board presidents are equipped to handle those responsibilities. And equipping them for important work brings gratitude and a better relationship, all the way around.

Hero makers establish the finest relationships with their board presidents by Teaching Up, so presidents are equipped with whatever they need to Teach Down and Teach Around. The cycle is ongoing—empowering, enlightening, and energizing.

Consensus Building

For optimal superintendent–board president relationships, hero makers lean into consensus building. What we mean here is recognizing when competing perspectives in one's community, or even on a school board, bring about conflict. There's a way to handle conflict resolution, and then there's a way not to handle it. Consensus building allows superintendents and board presidents to foster and maintain excellent relationships with each other, and others too, by leaning into the conflict energy and moving through productive struggle toward better outcomes on the other side of any issue faced. They find answers that everyone can live with. They do this by recognizing something rather unconventional in the life of schools, that's not often said:

Sometimes it is all about each individual board member first, if we want it to be all about the entire board *most*.

It is all about each individual board member first, if we want it to be all about the entire board *most*.

Individual attention is a big player in conflict outcomes, and thus in governance. Typically five to nine people (or more) have their internal emotions and motivational influences competing with their external professional demeanor, when current circumstances unduly impact something they care about. Superintendent–board president relations are fine-tuned at their best when they help adults face conflict together. They do this by working the problems from the inside out and realizing those board members they are having the most difficulty with can be their best success stories and closest allies.

Thus, focusing solely on the group and/or ignoring the subjective interaction each board member experiences would be ignoring one dangerous blind spot, said another way, a big elephant in the room. This understanding is where you as the hero maker alongside your board president can encourage better relationships and increase team performance and cohesiveness. This is where you forge your own best relationship with a united front—both of you AND the board members—against a problem you're struggling with… not against each other.

With your help in consensus building your board president needs to be the person in all board members' lives who ensures they end every conversation with you in a better space than when they began it.

Hero makers establishing wonderful relationships with board presidents know and learn together that what people appear to be on the outside might not actually be what they are on the inside. With a hero maker's help, our board presidents will unearth these discoveries to connect and make a difference, and will grow to appreciate all you are providing.

Befriending

Leaders are often asked if they'd rather be liked or respected, and the expected, acceptable response in educational administration circles, is to be respected. For optimal superintendent–board president relationships, hero makers acknowledge this advice yet also depart from it, just a bit. They recognize that liking one another comes in many different forms.

We offer the following:

- ◆ Wouldn't it be better if your board president looked forward to your weekly call?
- ◆ Isn't it a great thing if your board president walks away from the weekly conversation feeling better than before they took your call?
- ◆ Might it be a good thing if your board president remembered most of the details of what you discussed in your weekly connection, yet remembered ALL of how they felt, and all that was good in the exchange?

This is what we mean by befriending. You and your board president will be spending a lot of time, energy, and sometimes emotion navigating the nuances of leadership and governance and accentuating the positive in each other and your board and school system, with an expressed desire for each entity to establish healthy demarcation. Here's more: If we were to say to you, "You stay in your lane, and we'll stay in ours," that's sometimes a tough thing to say because of the risk of offending the other person. Yet, this is what we need to do if we want boards to do board-of-education things and superintendents to do superintendent things. We don't want, on our not-so-best days, to encroach on each other's natural roles and job descriptions.

Making friends with your board president is actually not a bad idea and does not cross a line, in terms of appropriate work friendships. Having "a friend at work" for each of you can help—your board president as your work friend, and you as theirs. But, of course it is not a requirement in any way. As authors Wilfong and Donlan (2024) note, workplace friendship is that which involves trust, commitment, values, and interests that go beyond merely knowing each other. We think your being open to a workplace friendship with your board president is helpful, natural, and mutually beneficial. Note with caution that this friendship does not include close caucusing against others on the board who may disagree with the both of you, but it could very well include caucusing against the problem you are all having. That's a healthy friendship.

***

As we have shared in our chapter here, a key ingredient in any hero making superintendency is the relationship between the superintendent and the board president. Positive relationships do not exist by chance. They are intentionally built and fed, if they are to remain vital and strong. It is with this in mind we propose a recipe for building such relationships, including key ingredients of perspective taking, targeting, respecting, connecting, navigating, equipping, consensus building, and befriending.

All of these ingredients are best used with careful attention to oneself first, as a hero maker.

✪ Hero-Making Tips

- Hero makers actively search inside and outside of the field of educational leadership for new ideas on how to relate to their board president—bringing out the hero in both the person and the role. They resist the temptation to think what they've seen in the past is the only way to navigate a superintendent–board president relationship; they do not discount this either, but remain open to a relationship do-over.
- Hero makers build positive relationships with their board president by helping them understand that negative board behavior can mask more positive intentions. Sometimes people's intentions are unrecognizable because of how they go about handling themselves when they are stressed or uncertain. In such cases, hero makers help their board president take active steps to leverage positive conflict energy to get at what the person is concerned about individually, to get them thinking collectively.
- Hero makers recognize that curating and maintaining the best relationship with their board president takes time, attention, and energy, and hero makers ensure they first attend to what they themselves need, so that they can bring out the best in the board president.

Reference

Wilfong, S., & Donlan, R. (2024). *Ensuring teachers matter: Where to focus first so students matter most*. Solution Tree Publishing.

9
Advancing, by Retreating

The last few chapters have talked about working with the school board on a regular basis—during regularly scheduled meetings and in between. These times are essential. There are also special events that are important. In our work with superintendents, boards, and school districts, we have many times noticed the value of time spent when the entire governance team comes together outside of the regular board meeting schedule. This has especially been true when we have facilitated school board retreats. Here are some observations we have made over the years:

Hero makers who facilitate the professional development of their boards through annual retreats provide two things that are very important: (1) an opportunity for board members to see and feel the experience of being a student of governance, while stepping away from their familiar boardroom dynamic, and (2) an opportunity for board members to get to know each other better personally, and to get to know their leaders better as hero makers as well.

Retreats can and do come in all shapes and sizes, and while we are not necessarily going to recommend one or another, we will stress the need to have all board members participate, if possible. In fact, having this as an expectation that the board president shares with members while they are candidates for election is

DOI: 10.4324/9781003613688-10

> **If the entire board does not commit to new learning together, each year, then they will have a much more difficult time making a positive difference through the responsibilities they embrace.**

important—in that if the entire board does not commit to new learning together, each year, then they will have a much more difficult time making a positive difference through the responsibilities they embrace. Boards need to stay current, and they must do this together.

We recommend the following considerations when planning for an annual retreat:

Location

Think about hosting the retreat somewhere that is actually close by, but feels far away—possibly a small conference building, cabins and rooms of various sizes, a restaurant, and trails to walk. You'll want it to have something for everyone: Public spaces, private spaces, and everything in-between.

You'll want each board member's travel time there to not be too long, yet when everyone arrives, it really does seem like you are far away from home. This may even keep some from leaving early.

Your retreat location can provide the necessary and deserved "vibe" or atmosphere, if you select wisely.

For optimal learning to occur, you and your board must be able to be wherever you are, in the moment, and feeling a bit special about being there as well. You want board members to take enough of a drive—separately or in groups—to be able to process what has been learned and experienced. You will want to be glad that they stepped away and feel like it was some time well-earned and well-spent by their service.

You will also want to ensure that whatever location you select, the people working at that location know who is coming from your board and why—and will work overboard to ensure your board feels special and important being there. Provide a photograph of your board with their names to the facility manager, and ask that their staff use board member names whenever possible (*Mr. So-&-So, Ms. So-&-So, Dr. So-&-So*, etc.).

Every detail that you can personalize or individualize in terms of comfort for your board—do it. This is particularly important in terms of environmental preferences. Some members prefer working and learning in groups, while others prefer to work and learn alone. Since the retreat will primarily be about group learning, you should ensure that time is also provided for board members to discuss training content in dyads if they wish, to take a stroll, to get some alone time intermittently, and even to text, send an email, or make a call or two, if they need to intermittently plug-in in order to unplug.

Itinerary

We strongly recommend hero makers consider the following options to divide-up time spent at an annual retreat: (1) board of education group goals and a focus on board business and school governance for the coming year; (2) training and professional development in stewardship, leadership, and governance; and (3) the superintendent's goals that the board will oversee.

Board Goals

Goals and a focus on board business and school governance are recommended in terms of a board's own vision and mission. This is the board's vision and mission, not the school district's. The vision is where the board ideally would like to arrive regarding its own work and governance at the end of a time period (one year, three years, five years); the mission is what they will focus on as they are attempting to get there (how they will behave, what they will discuss). It's important to discuss and clarify these goals because this is where hero makers can validate someone's pet project (or pet peeve) through transparent discussion, prioritization, and hopefully consensus. Whether or not the hero maker facilitates this discussion is best left to the local dynamic and the preferences of the board and board president.

Often, an outside facilitator can say things to the board that the superintendent cannot, regarding how they might reach consensus on the more challenging issues. The crux is that the board discusses what their priorities are for the upcoming year, and why individual members who allowed their goals to take a second seat in years past may need a bit more consideration this time, as they have deferred patiently while others have taken precedence. That is, if they are good ideas.

Professional Development

Training and professional development are necessary for boards to remain current with the issues the school district is facing, and allow board members to showcase themselves as lead learners. This is a great place for superintendents to provide a legislative or legal update, as well as new items from the state department of education. It is critical a hero maker never refers to "the state" as the bad guy or gives any impression local school districts are being victimized by some new law, edict, or policy.

Hero makers remain above the fray and do not whine.

Hero makers demonstrate to boards that although challenges come the way of local schools, *your* superintendent will remain in touch with policymakers and will continually put forth effort in educating them about the needs of your school district, and will showcase the phenomenal work that the teachers, students, and families are doing.

Consummate contextualizers, hero makers always turn challenge into opportunity, and have information on how the board's work will be critical as we navigate what lies ahead. Hero makers remain positive. This is where hero makers demonstrate good stewardship, as our best caretakers continually encourage, *Don't worry, be happy.*

Hero makers offer the impression, "Everything will be okay, as we have the A-team in school governance and the greatest community on earth."

At some point in the training and professional development portion of the day, the hero maker must step away from the podium and become a co-learner with the board. This is where everyone *goes to school* and learns something new.

The subject of "sound school governance" always has something valuable to cover that could be delivered through a great presenter in an hour or two. It is key for the hero maker to help with the lesson planning beforehand. There must be some goal or objective that the hero maker wants the board to learn—whether it is about relationships with one another, about the board's policymaking roles (without micromanagement), or about consensus building and conflict resolution. The new learning could be about community stewardship, about dealing with difficult people in the grocery store, or about work–life balance and how leaders must be comfortable with imbalance. It could be about myriad topics.

Our best hero makers use another's voice to reinforce a point that they want made to their board, so that their board becomes more like the kind of policymaking body the hero maker desires.

Superintendent Goals

Using the retreat as an opportunity to have an initial discussion of the goals the board has for the superintendent is also an annual necessity. The board president or another board member could facilitate this section of the retreat. An hour or so could be used for this purpose, as the aim is not to finalize the superintendent's goals at this juncture, but rather to talk about some possibilities and why they are important. This is not an evaluation of the superintendent; the retreat would not be an ideal place for this. Rather, the venue could include having the superintendent reflect on some of the expectations the board had of the superintendent the year prior, and what action was taken.

Hero makers use these discussions as an opportunity to plant seeds in the board members' minds regarding what they feel would be important, yet doing so in a way that gives the board the impression it was their idea, as in the following example:

> When I was talking with our board treasurer, Bob, recently, and got the impression that although last year was a great year in terms of adding to our fund equity, we all may benefit if I am more intentional in messaging locally how we are managing our finances. We almost have enough for a new stadium. I'm always open to any ideas you have, in terms of my goals, and I appreciated that being brought up, as I might not have thought as directly about it otherwise.

Takeaways

Effectively scheduled and delivered, a hero maker's retreat allows the board to see itself as responsible for doing something besides overseeing the school district. It provides a collective awareness that as a body, the members have the responsibility *to themselves* and others to remain headed in a direction that they collectively agree is important. This reduces ambiguity, uncertainty, and hopefully kneejerk reactions to the squeaky wheels always present with agendas falling outside the direction the board wishes to go.

> **Effectively scheduled and delivered, a hero maker's retreat allows the board to see itself as responsible for doing something besides overseeing the school district.**

The annual retreat provides an opportunity for the board members to grow and develop in their professional knowledge and leadership abilities, and as we have discussed, with an enhanced skill set of any kind, self-efficacy develops, in which one's increased confidence and self-concept increases the possibility that needs will be met positively, as opposed to negatively. It also provides the opportunity for the hero maker to share their appreciation for and willingness to embrace the goals the board has set, while also providing assurances if the board allows the superintendent as chief executive/operating officer to operationalize policy, it will be done with the board's authority and governance desires in mind. This may reduce micromanagement.

Finally, a hero maker's retreat provides a great opportunity for hero makers to treat board members like heroes—through location, service, and itinerary. People coming together with others can enhance everyone's desire to work as a team, and help them appreciate the time, talent, and treasures everyone brings to this leadership opportunity.

In short, hero makers assist boards in *advancing, by retreating*.

✪ Hero-Making Tips

- Hero makers ensure the care and feeding they provide board members between meetings are amplified by staff members working at the location of the annual retreat. They proactively contact location managers and share that this is what they expect in paying for the use of their facilities. And, they have a contact on site who will make things happen quickly behind the scenes, if the superintendent whispers in their ear.
- Hero makers with board approval might consider inviting their school attorneys to a portion or segment of their board retreat. Certainly, inviting your school attorney to your retreat when lunch is served or when an interesting professional development topic is presented goes a long way to forging a more personally respectful relationship—and it allows school attorneys to become more tuned-in to what the board is learning. Offers for co-learning might even save you a few dollars in billable hours through the kind gesture of valuing their conversation and presence in a more relaxed setting with everyone. Hero makers understand the school attorney (in most instances) is hired by the board and are thankful

for the opportunity to invite the attorney to spend time with them all, because of the generous service and opinion they provide, and to maintain the relationship.
- Hero makers ensure they provide board members options regarding the board's goals, as well as the superintendent's. This is not done so much to predetermine how the board will decide upon what to focus; rather, it is done so that the board will not have to think too hard while at the event. Board members can always offer additional goals at their pleasure, and these may be better and more palatable if they do not have to think too hard in the process.
- Hero makers offer ideas (plant seeds) a year in advance when they want something important from their board, such as extensions of their own contract or additional benefits in their compensation packages. This way, the board has time to mull it over and does not feel rushed or blindsided in the retreat setting.
- Hero makers refer to the learning gained on the retreats at future meetings, to deepen the understanding of all board members regarding the important topics of study.

10

Board Personalities

In the book *The Secret Solution: How One Principal Discovered the Path to Success* (Whitaker et al., 2013), some of the typical personalities we find employed in K–12 school buildings are depicted through parable. It is the story of Principal Roger Rookie at Anytown Middle School, with three groups of teachers: The Superstars, the Fence-Sitters, and the Bullies. Characters such as Sandy Starr, Edgar Sleeper, and Carl Chameleon are among the starring roles. Those who read the book tell us they really *do* have these characters in their schools.

Archetypes are everywhere. We see typical archetypes on boards of education as well.

Over the years, we have met Hank Hillbilly, Gabby Gossip, and Simon Suit. We often see Al Athletic and Braxton Bean Counter way too involved in sports and finances. Marge Micro gets elected after a superintendent becomes unpopular, while Larry Local is related to everyone on your support staff, and Yogi Union joins the board when teachers are upset.

What hero makers know about these roles is that while appearing rather predictable on the surface, something lies deeper within their personalities that influences what they say, what they do, and what they need.

Do you ever wonder why some conversations with board members are easy to have, and others feel like a tooth extraction? Similarly, isn't it true with some board members, you find that conversations lead to where you intended, and with others, the discussions often seem to take a wrong turn, even though you painstakingly prepared? With some conversations you feel better after having had them than you did going in, and with others, the opposite. Because of these circumstances, you might over time avoid having conversations with some of your board members, and they with you.

That is not at all productive.

Consider a metaphor regarding "doors" and our communication preferences inspired by the work of legendary psychologist Dr. Taibi Kahler (2008, 2015, with credit to the discoveries and work of Dr. Paul Ware as well). Let's pretend we all have a door that is our favorite door, and every time someone knocks on it, we hear the person, and we open it wide. Pretend we also have another door nailed shut, and we don't even hear when someone knocks. In our other doors, we can only hear the knocks part of the time. Communication occurs optimally through open doors (Kahler, 2008, 2015).

These are not just metaphors; in terms of our hero-making communication, we have doorways that are open and shut too, and so do our board members. These doors exist in our personalities. Sometimes we are "open" to what our board members are saying. Sometimes we are "closed," and vice versa. Our personalities, and our board members' personalities, provide us clues as to which doors we are using, and which doors we can use. The key to productive relationships and ongoing communication is to keep opening doors whenever possible to what is being said to us, even when we want to shut them.

How we do so, as hero makers, lies within our personality.

Consider the many things our personalities provide for us. Our personalities provide us with the preferred perceptions in how we view the world (thinking, feeling, etc.). They provide us with preferred communication and management styles, in terms of how we want others to relate to us (Kahler, 2008). Our personalities give us environmental preferences in how we want our workspaces arranged, and whether we want to work together in groups, in pairs, or alone (Kahler, 2008). They provide us with our primary motivation for doing what we do, which often has to do with being someone's hero, of course, and our personalities even provide us with certain psychological needs that if met, give us the energy to work with other people, even those very different from us (Kahler, 2008).

Yet personalities provide something else as well. While it is true that our personalities bring many positives to our leadership and service, it is also true our personalities bring certain blind spots, causing us at times to come across to others in a way we cannot see.

Board members are no exception, and we recall from previous chapters it is a hero maker's job to function as the Shield to those board members who are unaware of how they are being perceived. Hero makers can use their knowledge of personality to cultivate new ways to operate which can protect their board members from the unanticipated consequences of their blind spots.

> **Hero makers can use their knowledge of personality to cultivate new ways to operate which can protect their board members from the unanticipated consequences of their blind spots.**

Consider the overly persistent questioning from a board member that could result in your best local contractor pulling out of a great bid that would have provided the safest playground equipment. Consider the insensitivity perceived in a board member that could tip the scales toward a parent filing a frivolous lawsuit. Consider the board member who frequently seems to focus on what is wrong, rather than what is good about something.

Over time, what is the effect?

Public dissatisfaction, of course. Employee discontent as well.

Hero makers who study personality provide both "saves" and "assists" to board members for better outcomes. They are better Shields.

We all have experienced conversations at board meetings in which board members can become critical, suspicious, defiant, manipulative, mistake-prone, or timid (Donlan, 2015). Fascinating is that these behaviors are predictable and avoidable. When board members behave as such, it is an advertisement that a hero maker's attention is needed, with knowledge and an understanding of one's *personality*.

Without such attention, we will see drama escalate in which all involved can play the roles of perpetrator, victim, and rescuer. A drama triangle (Karpman, 2014)!

Have we ever had drama at board meetings?

What is fascinating (yet worrisome) is that those involved in drama perform a predictable dance, and it is at times a more natural feeling to join the dance than to decline the invitation. In the dance of the drama triangle (Karpman, 1968, 2014; Regier & King, 2013), persecutors often seek out victims, and victims tend to oblige them. Victims look for rescuers, and rescuers are drawn to them. Rescuers keep a watch for persecutors as well, and when they find them, they will find victims to save. The dance begins, and continues on.

It's a true relationship of co-dependency.

Consider the community member with a mousy look on her face and a whiny sound in her voice (potentially rehearsed, but possibly not even with her awareness), reporting to the board that her child is getting picked on by your "nasty high school assistant principal." Singled-out, of course! Envision the board member helicoptering in and mentioning to the parent that the board will "take care of that."

The dance is on, starring: The Victimized Parent (and child), and in absentia the Prosecutorial Assistant Principal and, of course, at 500 feet descending with harness dangling… the Rescuing Board Member.

Drama provides first a curtsy, then a full-blown embrace, as it begins to move around the triangle, yet hero makers can stop it before the dance starts. They recognize when the music is about to begin, and with an understanding of personality can circumvent it.

One takeaway regarding board personalities is we cannot really change the hardwiring of others, so we might as well learn to connect with it. Doing so will bring out the best in board members' personalities, as hero makers know where to provide open doors of communication.

> **One takeaway regarding board personalities is we cannot really change the hardwiring of others, so we might as well learn to connect with it.**

As we began our chapter, we envisioned the archetypal board personalities of Hank Hillbilly, Gabby Gossip, and Simon Suit. Looking at their unique individualities is what personality analysis allows us, as it might reveal that Al Athletic and Braxton Bean Counter can focus their positive energy on other things besides sports and our fund balance. We might not be able to stop Marge Micro from requesting itemized receipts from the elementary candy sales, Larry Local from hosting yet another family wedding with all invited except you, or Yogi Union from holding court in his weekly coffee klatch, yet we can make inroads to better conversations through consideration of this story that began over 40 years ago, one that has inspired personality analysis worldwide.

In the late 1960s, while working as a clinical intern in a mental health treatment center, Taibi Kahler began making some innovative psychological discoveries. A theory he developed shortly thereafter earned him the Eric Berne Memorial Scientific Award from the International Transactional Analysis Association for the most impressive scientific discovery of the year (Kahler, 2008). This award was conferred with the support of 10,000 of Taibi's colleagues in 52 countries, so his work has attracted worldwide attention.

A few years later, NASA's leading psychiatrist for manned spaceflight, Dr. Terry McGuire, was working to enhance the American Space Program's astronaut selection processes. In learning of Taibi Kahler's work, he found that this specific theory could predict how astronauts would work with others in handling the rigors of spaceflight (Kahler, 2008).

Through further research and work with NASA, Dr. Kahler refined his developing models of personality and communication, finding applications in the corporate, therapeutic, and governmental sectors. During the years following, Dr. Kahler expanded his model's applications to non-profit service, health care, the spiritual, and education.

In the early 1990s, the United States National Democratic Committee asked Dr. Kahler to serve as a psycho-demographer in the presidential campaign of William Jefferson Clinton. President Clinton also received training in the model (Kahler, 2008). The Process Communication Model® (PCM) is now used worldwide to make a positive difference in people's lives in terms of leading, teaching, and learning.

We think PCM can help hero makers encourage positive relations and productivity in your board members as well.

✪ Hero-Making Tips

- Hero makers "find the pearl" in board members' personalities to forge a connection and recognize how to nurture that to a new level of closeness and mutual respect. That hillbilly on our board might be a member of American Mensa or Mensa International.
- Hero makers understand anytime we are in proximity with those who are different from us, it takes a great deal of energy to understand them, let alone tolerate their idiosyncrasies. One way to build up our energy is to spend appropriate time working to meet our own psychological needs. Key is to learn what they are, and then once we do, whether other people can charge our batteries, or whether we need to take on this responsibility ourselves. That's one way to find the pearl noted above.
- Hero makers first strive to understand their own personalities and especially their own blind spots, to determine how they might behave while under pressure and to have the capacity to connect with people different from them.

- Hero makers realize that when board members are in the dance of drama, it is more difficult to tactfully refuse, rather than to accept, the invitation. Staying out of drama takes practice, patience, and persistence. It's surprising how verbal and non-verbal responses we offer daily can dial-up drama, even when we don't intend this. Examples would be when we eagerly nod, affirm, or even "one-up" the details of a board member's complaining, as opposed to calmly acknowledging their personal challenge and offering a professional ear.
- Hero makers understand if they must ask board members to stretch the capabilities of the talents they bring to the board, then they must first focus on where people are naturally strong. This is like exercising the good leg to rehabilitate the other.

References

Donlan, R. (2015, January). The power of "process" for superintendents. *New Superintendents E-Journal*. American Association of School Administrators.

Kahler, T. (2008). *The Process Therapy Model: The six personality types with adaptations*. Taibi Kahler Associates.

Kahler, T. (2015). *The Process Communication Model® seminar: Seminar one/core topics*. Kahler Communications.

Karpman, S. B. (1968). Fairy tales and script drama analysis. *Transactional Analysis Bulletin* 26(7), 39–43.

Karpman, S. B. (2014). *A game-free life: The definitive book on the drama triangle and the compassion triangle by the originator and author*. Drama Triangle Publications.

Regier, N., & King, J. (2013). *Beyond drama: Transcending energy vampires*. Next Element Publishing.

Whitaker, T., Miller, S., & Donlan, R. (2013). *The secret solution: How one principal discovered the path to success*. Rowman & Littlefield Education.

11

Starting Undefeated

Education is such an unusual profession. There are clear starting points—the first day of school and other equally well-defined finish lines—the final day of school, graduation, etc. Typically, most new faculty members start their jobs on a certain date in a predetermined month which allows for some consistency in establishing expectations for the group. These situations allow for natural changes and growth. If we add 20 or 2,000 new employees all at once, we bring in a potential jolt of new ideas and energy. The enthusiasm level starts high, and the energy is palpable. This is a chance to bring about significant change.

Principals can establish differing expectations for teachers and students than were in place the previous year. Teachers can tweak the way they arrange the furniture, handle their classroom management practices, or refine their instruction.

This same opportunity arises for the superintendent.

The beginning of the year is a special time. Many districts have opening sessions where all employees get together and the excitement can be felt. Other professions are not accorded this opportunity. Imagine how difficult it is to build enthusiasm in a regular business office where every day feels the same. May is like November; Tuesday is like Friday.

> **A district leader has a chance to reestablish expectations and relationships on an annual or even perennial basis.**

A district leader has a chance to reestablish expectations and relationships on an annual or even perennial basis. For example, they have the ability to redouble their efforts to be more a mediator of perspectives than an information disseminator, if they wish. They can refine their efforts to weigh all (or more) sides of an issue before making decisions, as well as to balance more earnestly the interests of board members, community constituents, and educators. They can spend more time learning about student perspectives, we hope.

Of particular importance might be their opportunity (or obligation) to start undefeated on those things close to them, such as loved ones, family, personal relationships, and attending to their own interests and rejuvenation. We might caution that if these things fall apart or are left wanting, so might be the superintendency.

Each school year, hero makers can start undefeated and reestablish.

Although certain things may have occurred that make reestablishing and relationships more challenging, the start of the year provides new hope. This same opportunity can be there for board relations. There are elections, new officers, and the beginning of each school year that can allow for changes in practices. However, the best chance we will have as hero makers is when we first start in the role. This is especially true if when we start as superintendent, we are also new to the district.

The First Day of School

We often hear teachers must earn students' respect, but actually that is not true. Students usually behave very well the first day of school. Teachers are given that gift. What they do with it is up to them.

This same thing applies to principals. When they are first appointed, teachers dress better, and everyone is on time for the first meeting. What the principal does from that point forward determines if there will be a new norm, or if some teachers will quickly revert to arriving late for meetings and dressing more unprofessionally than we might wish. The principal had that window, as brief as might have been, to alter the school quickly and effectively.

Superintendents are also given that gift. Often when we are first hired, board members are on their best behavior. They are doing their thing with politeness so they can impress their new hire and make sure they get on their good side. This is an incredible opportunity for superintendents that they may not have again. This group came together and chose *you*. They want you to help them lead the school district. You were their choice. Now is the time to establish roles with the group.

If you did this during the interview, that is very powerful, but you still need to make sure these things are established while all are still smiling. This is never done in a directive or offensive way, of course. Many examples of how to word things, what language to use, etc., have been shared in previous chapters. But if you miss this window, it may never reopen. You are helping your board members to be heroes by teaching them how to function and interact with the public, with each other, and with you.

Think of it as the first day on the job.

When you first walk into the office, your administrative assistant wants to know how you want them to answer the phone. They want to please the new boss. However, they only want to know how to answer the phone up until the point when they actually answer the phone. Then your administrative assistant no longer wants to know how to answer. Because at this point you are correcting their behavior; you are no longer establishing how you hope things will go. Everyone wants to know the rules of the game before they start playing. Unless they plan to cheat. And the better they are the more they want to know the rules. So, the best thing you can do is provide them with the guidelines and expectations so they can avoid a misstep.

This is the same dynamic with your board.

They chose you. They want you to succeed.

Now is the best opportunity to help provide guidance for them on how to best make that happen. If it doesn't happen now, when will it?

A similar opportunity is available with new board members. Meeting with candidates before the election can be a great time to help build a relationship, and it can also be a time to help them understand how to be most effective in their potential new role. Meeting with all candidates is key, in order not to show preference. Neutrality is key! Obviously once the new candidates are elected or appointed, it becomes imperative to help provide them the guidance you both need to be successful. If there is a board president or individual member who can assist with this, that may be beneficial, but it is critical you work to make sure the relationship starts off on as productive of a note as possible. You might also meet with those who were not elected, to thank them for their desire to serve.

> Our roles are so complex that we can never stay undefeated in the eyes of everyone for very long. But regardless, we must do what is right. That is the only thing that always works out in the long run.

Our roles are so complex that we can never stay undefeated in the eyes of everyone for very long. But regardless, we must do what is right. That is the only thing that always works out in the long run.

It would be nice if the community agrees with every decision we make. It would be wonderful if the school board agrees with every decision we make. It is essential that we agree with every decision we make.

⭐ Hero-Making Tips

- Hero makers realize that their first "at-bat" is their only *first* at-bat. They still can make home runs for the rest of their career, but they will not again have an opportunity to make a home run on their first at-bat.
- Hero makers realize that their leadership has a grade-point average, just like students have grade-point averages in

school. They know that their earlier grades from board members will have much more of an impact on their leadership tenure (grade-point-average), because earlier grades weigh-in more significantly. And even though board members tend to focus on the here and how, those things that superintendents do later on will have not as big of an impact on their overall job-performance grade, as they try to catch up.
- Hero makers realize that at the end of a day, week, semester, or school year, they will not remain completely undefeated, so it is important to maintain honor in the way they play the game of leadership. After all, each player inducted into any given sports hall of fame had a win/loss record that included some losses. Those are what define our greatest hero makers.
- Hero makers are eager to embrace the reality that "Dog Years" works in tandem with this whole notion of "Starting Undefeated." This is explained more in our next chapter, The Tour of Duty.

12

The Tour of Duty

Is there an optimal length of a superintendent's tour of duty in one location? Donlan and Gruenert (2016) asked this of school building leaders when they envisioned an actuarial table, in terms of dog years, in their book *Minds Unleashed: How Principals Can Lead the Right-Brained Way*. How about those leading at the district level?

Using the helpful information as the authors did from www.dogyears.com, we offer the following:

TABLE 12.1 Comparison of Dog Years to Human Years

Dog Years	*Human Years*
1 year old	15 years old
2 years old	24 years old
3 years old	28 years old
4 years old	32 years old
5 years old	37 years old
6 years old	42 years old
7 years old	47 years old
8 years old	52 years old
9 years old	57 years old
10 years old	62 years old

Source: Information provided at www.dogyears.com (retrieved for 2nd Edition, June 23, 2025).

The authors offered some metaphorical parallels that we'll build on here in terms of hero making (Donlan & Gruenert, 2016).

In leadership's first year, does one have the hero-making maturity of a 15-year-old (Donlan & Gruenert, 2016), thinking one knows all the answers? The authors mention both insecurity and overconfidence, which could impede hero making without mentorship.

In leadership's third year, does one have the hero-making maturity of a 28-year-old (Donlan & Gruenert, 2016)? The authors mentioned knowing what one wants at this age, which we believe is a hero-making asset.

In leadership's fifth year, does one have the hero-making maturity of a 37-year-old (Donlan & Gruenert, 2016)? We feel these are primetime opportunities for hero making, as the district starts to embody the values of a superintendent.

In leadership's tenth year, does one have the hero-making maturity of a 62-year-old (Donlan & Gruenert, 2016)? The authors mention wisdom, which can be employed judiciously in the creation of heroes.

Is there a time when it is simply best that superintendents move to another location, so they can put some more vim and vigor into their leadership?

We would like to ask the following: Is there a time when it is simply best that superintendents move to another location, so they can put some more vim and vigor into their leadership? Of course, we realize that some move for other reasons, such as the desire for a new challenge or to live in another locale with family.

With that acknowledged, should hero makers from time to time have a "re-do" on their hero making?

Does the superintendency have an optimal tour-of-duty lifespan?

Consider what a tour of duty involves.

In an ideal tour of duty in leadership and governance of a school district, everyone would know their roles and a well-oiled machine would be moving toward educational excellence with almost military precision. Boards would set policy, establish the budget, evaluate the hero maker from time to time, but most of all, get out of the way of daily operations.

Superintendents would do their part as well, leading the business of schools, finding the best talent to deploy, then managing, teaching, and supporting those at the building level, and most important, tending to the relationships between themselves and their boards, so that this fine chorus of activity moves forward, uninterrupted.

In terms of an optimal tour of duty, we now share what might happen in key roles on an annual basis, so that one school season builds on the last, and moves effortlessly into the next. We want all in an educational community to experience continuous improvement in which a superintendent's tenure is one in which there's only one driver in the driver's seat—the hero maker.

An optimal tour of duty involves the superintendent serving in eight key roles as any given year progresses: (1) superintendent as concierge; (2) superintendent as lead learner; (3) superintendent as vision-gatherer; (4) superintendent as consensus builder; (5) superintendent as quality-assurance provider; (6) superintendent as steward; (7) superintendent as responsibility taker; and (8) superintendent as meaning maker.

Superintendent as Concierge welcomes new members to the board, provides them information on how to make their stay as comfortable as possible, offers directions to anything that might bolster sustenance and nourishment, and generally offers an ever-attentive presence where "Nothing is a problem, as asked," and "No question is too big or too small." Key to this role is that hero makers strive to offer more positive attention to the new board members upon arrival than the negative faction will. You want to provide the security and supports so that they know your door is open and they want to have lunch with the right board members, those who have your best interests and the students' best interests at heart.

Superintendent as Lead Learner is one who, through example, models an annual willingness (summer retreat or otherwise) to step away from their comfort zone and learn something new that might benefit their leadership, the group's governance, or the district's ability to learn and educate. This lead learner not only amasses increasing knowledge regarding the technical aspects of institutional leadership, but also focuses on people management. Through their reading, research, and willingness to step outside their comfort zones, hero makers demonstrate their ability to recognize when to do things differently and make changes that are difficult for them. Think of it this way: When board members resist changes you are making (because they are uncomfortable with them), you want them to understand this may be a sign they have an opportunity to grow and enjoy the learning involved. You can't expect them to think and analyze things; they must see them and feel them to become true believers. For board members to be comfortable with discomfort, they must witness vicariously the fact that you are benefiting from it, and that you are reflecting on the good it has done you.

> **For board members to be comfortable with discomfort, they must witness vicariously the fact that you are benefiting from it, and that you are reflecting on the good it has done you.**

Superintendent as Vision Gatherer is one who can reach deeply and authentically into the minds and hearts of those assembled on the board to hear what is important to them, to validate what they bring in terms of passion and perspective. One of the most important skills of a hero maker is the ability to take ideas that are complex and simplify them in a way that brings people together with a concrete understanding of what is going on and in a way they can simply and quickly relay to constituents why they support your vision. Key is your ability to use metaphor in line with each board member's interests, aptitudes, and abilities. One vision may take seven or eight metaphors to explain—a general metaphor for the group and an individual one for each board member.

> **One of the most important skills of a hero maker is the ability to take ideas that are complex and simplify them in a way that brings people together.**

Superintendent as Consensus Builder is one who can begin the hard work of helping board members prioritize their opinions for the school district into a smart, workable policy and budgetary allocation plan for the year, where "all can live with that." Key to this role is a hero maker's ability to allow all board members to have a voice, with enough time so that they are satisfied that they have been heard. Donlan and Gruenert (2016) note a technique gleaned from consensus-building specialist Bob Chadwick from Consensus Associates. The superintendent or board president during a work session would ask each board member to share their perspective or "pass," moving from one to the next. Each would share uninterrupted and without debate. Important is for the facilitator to move around the boardroom table a second time, so that those who are more introverted (or those who may have "passed") can have time to reflect and offer something the next time around. Techniques such as these forge consensus and buy-in.

Superintendent as Quality-Assurance Provider is one who is relied on to keep a close look over the resources allocated by the board. It involves delegating smartly but only to those persons who have the willingness and capability to exercise talent on behalf of the public's trust. Quality-assurance providing also involves anticipating problems before they surface rather than playing whack-a-mole with things not anticipated. It involves keeping the board president in the loop and seeking their perspective weekly. It also involves pulling triggers on ideas and terminating employees who let the district down. If the business of schools is not being run effectively… then no amount of curricular leadership is going to keep a superintendent in a position to wield influence as a hero maker.

> **If the business of schools is not being run effectively… then no amount of curricular leadership is going to keep a superintendent in a position to wield influence as a hero maker.**

Superintendent as Steward means serving through any given year as one who is trusted and approachable. Stewarding involves much more listening than talking, with a careful balance of deliberating and acting. It involves not always giving people what they want, yet rather providing people what they need to grow.

A steward is one who cares for the good of the whole, as well as the good of all parts in the whole. The best stewards know "It is people, not programs," that make a difference, and know that adults' capacities in schools must be leveraged *first*, if school is going to be about children *most*.

Superintendent as Responsibility Taker accepts full responsibility for *everything* that goes badly in the entire school district and gives credit away for everything that goes well. This can be an arduous demand on superintendents and something hard to swallow, as some school districts are as complicated as small (or large) municipalities, and many things can occur outside of superintendents' awareness (extramarital affairs in the office, embezzlement, and instructional neglect, to name a few). Hero makers find ways to develop organizational acuity so that more things are in their line of vision, as opposed to outside of it. They then feel comfortable embracing ambiguity and uncertainty—and dealing with it.

Finally, *Superintendent as Meaning Maker* finds a way to take an entire year's worth of experience and information, and *make meaning* in terms of what they report to the board. Key is for hero makers to unearth the value in what the board has done in terms of governance. This is especially true in policy work, as often these efforts do not reap immediate gratification. It is important the hero maker finds ways to allow the board to make meaning of times when it does the right thing, staying within its role—in the marathon while avoiding the sprint. It involves teaching board members how to make meaning for their constituencies, so that all will be satisfied and each board member will be seen as a hero.

Each of these tasks is possible and all-important for hero makers, so that both boards of education and communities are satisfied, with continued calisthenics in the making of heroes. Calisthenics, one might say, starts with reading this book.

No one size fits all, but it sure is more fun to go to work when you are excited to be there and feel you are well-placed in that regard.

Every leader does need to examine their own circumstance and energy in deciding which of the roles above to prioritize, and at what times (when). We all have strengths and weaknesses. No one size fits all, but it sure is more fun to go to work when you are excited to be there and feel you are well-placed in that regard. That is why you chose the job you did, so it also needs to be part of the reason you stay.

So, we ask the same questions here as we did in the beginning of this chapter: Is there a time when it is simply best that superintendents move to another location, so that they can put some more vim and vigor into their leadership? Should hero makers from time to time have a "re-do" on their hero making?

Our belief is that when a superintendent wanes in either the ability *or interest* of serving "energetically" in the roles described, then an actuary might be tapping on one's shoulder. It might then be time to consider that closing the current door of district-level service might open another window of opportunity, for both the superintendent and the community.

✪ Hero-Making Tips

- Hero makers are honest when they look in the mirror and reflect on their actuarial table. They don't crane their neck or put on too much hair color. They make an honest appraisal of their "dog years" and are not hesitant to ask someone they trust who is candid with feedback.
- Hero makers recognize if their desire is to be career-bound, or place-bound. As we learned from the research of Dr. David Hoffert (2014), this is important because one's bound-ness has implications for leadership and decisions. Unchecked, this can lead to bias in decision making, so hero makers ask a trusted confidant to keep close watch on their blind spots.
- Hero makers teach their boards that just as superintendents might have actuarial tables, boards of education possibly do as well. Sometimes the length of a board member's service can adversely impact perspective, if disenchanted with the challenges faced or disinterested in topics that reach the board's attention time and again. This is best discussed in good times, not in bad.

♦ Hero makers, when they exit for new pursuits, work to leave the schools and the board of education in better places than they found them upon arrival.

References

Donlan, R., & Gruenert, S. (2016). *Minds unleashed: How principals can lead the right-brained way*. Rowman & Littlefield Education.

Hoffert, D. A. (2014). *Finding the correct fit or quickly finding an exit for school superintendents: Perceptions from those who placed them or are commissioned to replace them*. Doctoral Dissertation, Indiana State University

Epilogue

What Next? Toward "Difference-Making"

So, you are probably getting pretty good, or you were already very good, at hero making. We are glad to offer what we can so that you can have outstanding—or at least professional—relationships with your board, as you lead and serve on behalf of the children in your schools.

Make no mistake about it. You are leading and serving to leverage the best governance in your board members, for a purpose.

So they can *"make a difference,"* of course.

You see, as you close this book, something else will happen around you. If you look closely enough, you will see opening up a window of opportunity.

It's a whole new day!

Your hero making allows you the opportunity to develop your board members' best selves to make a difference, not just for your students, families, leadership teams, and community, but also for your board members. This can last beyond your leadership tenure, and here is why.

We have already shared board members can become hero makers, too. In fact, this is one of your greatest teachable moments: Showing them how. Once doing that, the investment reaps dividends as those who know and communicate with board members feel like heroes; in turn the board members' needs are being met (as they are heroes); and when everyone is feeling pretty good, it is much easier to put the collective brainpower into problem solving, planning, and even preventing issues from coming our way.

It is like a performance-enhancing supplement for ensuring everyone brings their A-game to the relationships you have and to the important work you are trying to accomplish.

You all have a better ability to make a difference, once board members are hero-made, than before they wore that title.

The Difference Maker

Consider this: Your core incentive to becoming a teacher was to make a difference. Then you became a school-level leader to have even more of an impact. Eventually, you became a district-level leader to have even more of a positive influence on students. Even if you did not take the specific path just described, you have arrived at the same point. You do not want simply to make time pass or get through another school year.

You want to make a difference. That is what is at the core of each of our educator's souls.

We are not just in education for the money and glory (that was supposed to be funny, by the way). We have chosen to be educators to affect generations, way beyond our own. We aim to leave a legacy that lasts far beyond our working years. So does almost everyone else who is in our profession. What we must do is to help align being a hero with doing the right thing. By choosing the correct path, we will feel and be more valued than if we choose a *look-at-me* or less-important road. Once people internalize these connections, they then can focus solely on making a difference.

Not for them, but for others.

That is why we chose education.

That is why we choose to lead.

We want to make a difference. We want to have a positive impact for years to come.

Just as we teach others how to become heroes, we also must provide the path for others to be difference makers. At the end of the day, we know we are in the right profession when we look in the mirror and see that tired face and realize what we do really matters.

It reminds us of the story leaders share when they say they only hire people better than themselves.

Lots of people say it.

Few people do it.

Many are too threatened to really seek out talent. Ironically, rather than hiring people better than ourselves in a holistic way, we typically are seeking those who are more talented or knowledgeable than we are in a specific area. It may be technology, curriculum, or special education. Whatever it is, if leaders consistently hire truly outstanding people, they have not hired anyone more talented than they are. Because selecting and attracting excellence may be the best talent there is.

We also must reflect on the fact that every time we arrange for someone to be a hero, we become more of one ourselves. Inviting other people to feel like a hero allows them to see you as one.

Perhaps that is our greatest gift. Making heroes. Making a difference.

Thanks for doing both. Our students deserve it.

For Product Safety Concerns and Information please contact our EU
representative GPSR@taylorandfrancis.com
Taylor & Francis Verlag GmbH, Kaufingerstraße 24, 80331 München, Germany

www.ingramcontent.com/pod-product-compliance
Lightning Source LLC
Chambersburg PA
CBHW070404240426
43661CB00056B/2526